How Animals Move

J. H. PRINCE

How Animals Move

ELSEVIER/NELSON BOOKS
New York

Library of Congress Cataloging in Publication Data

Prince, J. H. (Jack Harvey).
  How animals move.

  Includes index.
  Summary: Explains the basic principles of
movement of vertebrates and insects: swimming,
running and walking, flying and gliding, and
undulating or wriggling.
  1. Animal locomotion. [1. Animal locomotion]
I. Title.
QP301.P74   1981   591.1′852   81-815
ISBN 0-525-66712-1   AACR2

Published in the United States by Elsevier-Dutton Publishing Co., Inc.,
2 Park Avenue, New York, N.Y. 10016. Published simultaneously in Canada
by Clarke, Irwin & Company Limited, Toronto and Vancouver

Printed in the U.S.A.   First Edition
10 9 8 7 6 5 4 3 2

Contents

How Animals Move

Introduction

All living things are capable of movement. Apart from their natural growth, even plants can be seen to move when watched through speeded-up time-lapse photography. Plants respond to the influences of sun, temperature, wind, and moisture. When we speak of movement in animals, however, we are thinking more of movement from one place to another or of the use of limbs, joints, and muscles.

The subject of movement in animals is so vast that in this book I will consider only limbs and body-propelling movements in higher animals, ignoring the probing movements of tiny organisms like amoebas, and the cilia-controlled movements of so many other microorganisms. To avoid making even that restricted subject matter too cumbersome, the vertebrates alone will be discussed, together with the various patterns of flight found in insects.

Although vertebrates have many patterns of movement, and various means with which these are accomplished, we are accustomed to dividing them into four main categories: swimming, running and walking, flying and gliding, and undulating or wriggling as in snakes and snake-lizards. There is considerable overlapping in these groups—fish that glide, and others that walk; birds that swim, and others that do not fly; mammals that hop and can never walk, and others that hang in trees.

1

Most of these patterns of locomotion are the result of animals' choosing particular ways of life, environments, or food; others have been evolved to escape particular enemies. Patterns of movement are always involved with survival, escape from enemies, capturing prey, moving to new areas of available food, or in response to climatic conditions.

Part I

GENERAL PRINCIPLES
OF LOCOMOTION

Chapter 1

THE MECHANICS
OF LIMB MOVEMENT

Limb movement is produced by the action of muscles located in or attached to movable parts of the body. There are three factors involved in the effort these muscles must exert: the weight they must move, the speed with which they must operate, and the frequency with which they must function. Muscle-power output depends on size (length and bulk), an efficient supply of oxygen and nutrients, temperature, and the nature of the animal's metabolic activity.

When vertebrates of all kinds are compared, it is found that, however much they differ in size, shape, and manner of life, they are built on the same general plan. In the forelimbs of vertebrates, for instance, there is a general pattern of bones that is similar whether the animal is a bird, a frog, a reptile, or a mammal; or whether it lives in water, on land, or in the air. At certain embryonic stages the similarities are even greater than in the mature animals.

Muscles

There are generally more than six hundred muscles to control conscious movement in the body of an average animal the size of a dog or cat, or larger, and there are many others that are involved with

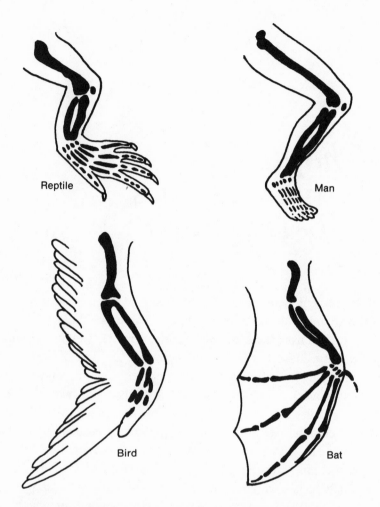

1. Whatever the animal—fish, amphibian, reptile, bird, or mammal—the same basic bone structure is present. These bones may be of grossly different proportions, or may have been sacrificed in embryonic development.

unconscious movements. Those that operate voluntary movements, such as walking or manipulating objects, are known as *voluntary* or *striated* (striped) muscles, and it is the action of these that generates most of the body's heat. Movements that occur without conscious effort, such as digestion, heartbeat, artery pulsation, and focusing the eyes, are made by *involuntary* or *smooth* (plain or unstriped) muscles.

The action of muscles is through contraction and relaxation, but muscles are seldom completely relaxed. They are normally in a state of slight tension called *tonus,* neither slack nor taut, just slightly tensed so that they are ready for action. Individual muscle fibers, however, are always completely relaxed or fully contracted. There is no intermediate stage. The whole muscle is therefore slightly tense because it always has some contracted and some relaxed fibers. In sudden action, all the relaxed fibers contract. The degree of contraction of all these muscles is about half their relaxed length.

Those muscles concerned with maintaining posture show considerably more tonus than those that come into action only when an animal decides to move them. Each muscle is really a separate organ controlled by a special nerve or nerves, which connects with the spinal cord and brain and which stimulates the muscle to contract as dictated by the brain.

The striated voluntary muscles are made up of long fibers showing alternate light and dark bands of a special form of *contractile protoplasm*. Each fiber is enclosed in a delicate sheath, the *sarcolemma,* and varies in length from a few millimeters to a foot, according to

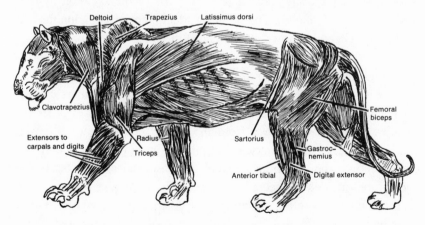

2. *The immense size of some of the muscles serving the limbs of a lion can be clearly seen in this diagram.*

the size of the animal. The fibers are bound together by connective tissue to form bundles (*fasciae*), and the bundles massed together form the various voluntary muscles.

Several muscles are needed to carry out even a simple movement. One or more act as *prime movers,* or *protagonists,* and contract; while others, called *opponents* or *antagonists,* relax at that time. Although every muscle has been named, there is no point in listing them or discussing them individually now, since we are only concerned with the way they are involved with movement.

So far as mammals are concerned, there are likely to be up to fifty-eight muscles involved in the operation of each forelimb and close to the same number in a rear limb. In addition to these, movement is dependent on many muscles in the trunk and neck, and some in the abdominal area, so that even the process of walking slowly is a very complex one. For an all-out effort at escape or capture, the power output when compared to the weight of the particular animal is likely to be immense.

Tendons

Most voluntary muscles are attached to parts of the skeleton by *tendons,* also called *sinews.* The point of attachment of a tendon nearest the trunk or head is known as its *origin;* the other end is its *insertion.* Some muscles have more than one origin, and so will have correspondingly more tendons to anchor them.

Tendons consist of bands of strong, nonelastic white fibers continuous with the sarcolemmal sheaths of the muscle fibers. In order for muscles to act at a distance from the bone, tendons must often be quite long. The many muscles required for complicated multiple movements of the thumb and fingers, for instance, are located in the upper forearm, and connected with the *digits* or *fingers* by long, thin tendons. In this way the hands can be given strength without bulky muscles in them, so that the fingers can be both nimble and retain their full power and coordination.

Tendons also permit changes in the direction of a muscle's pull, since they can turn around a bony prominence such as a knee or elbow. But they are often subjected to considerable friction at the turning point, and special protection is provided in the form of small *sesamoid* bones or fibrous pouches. The term "sesamoid" has been adopted for these bones because they have the shape of sesame seeds.

Bones and Cartilage

These structures form the entire framework on which the body is built. Many of them are fixed, but most are hinged, so that the body shape can be changed by the action of the muscles that produce movement. Bones obtain their strength and rigidity by being made up of a combination of fibrous tissue, phosphate, and carbonate of lime, but too high a proportion of carbonate of lime makes them too brittle: Young animals have a higher proportion of fibrous tissue in their bones than old ones, and this is one of the factors in their suppleness.

Bone that makes up the shafts of large limbs is often called *dense* bone because it is hard. Dense bone forms a tube containing *marrow,* a fatty substance also present within the meshwork that forms smaller and shorter bones and the ends of the long ones. This kind of bone is called *cancellous.* The marrow is very important, since the red corpuscles of the blood are formed there.

Around bones is a membrane, the *periosteum,* which contains the blood vessels and nerves that nourish the bone within, and these extend through fine canals within the bone itself. Another important structure related to bone is a tissue known as *cartilage.* This is a hard but flexible material containing no nerves or blood vessels, which forms a cushion between the moving ends of connected bones to reduce friction. Cartilage surrounds the entire ends of some bones, where it plays a part in bone formation during growth.

The skeleton of a walking animal averages about two hundred bones. Three kinds of bones are involved in limb function: long ones in the form of shafts, short ones that give the wrists and ankles their flexibility, and the irregular vertebrae of the spine.

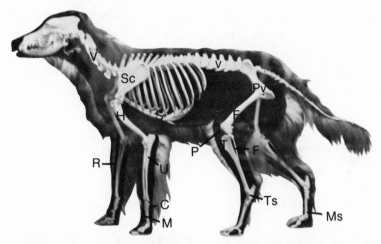

3. *The skeleton of a dog showing the important bones in the limbs.* C, *carpals;* F, *fibula;* Fe, *femur;* H, *humerus;* M, *metacarpals;* Ms, *metatarsals;* P, *patella;* Pv, *pelvis;* R, *radius;* S, *sternum;* Sc, *scapula;* T, *tibia;* Ts, *tarsals;* U, *ulna;* V, *vertebrae.*

A forelimb includes a shoulder region and three segments: an upper arm, forearm, and wrist with a hand or paw, all the segments being separated from each other by joints. A hind limb consists similarly of a haunch or side of the pelvis and three segments: thigh, leg, and foot. It is much the same in a bird, but a fish has many fin rays instead. It also has many more ribs than a land animal.

Ligaments

Unlike tendons, ligaments are not part of the muscular structure. They are tough fibrous bands developed at joints to keep bones together. Other ligaments form slings to hold tendons at the shoulder, wrist, and ankle joints. At the knee, a small bone develops in the substance of the tendon of the large muscle that extends the leg, the *quadriceps femoris,* and this protects the muscle from friction at the bend of the knee. Bones of this kind also occur under toe joints and in other similar areas.

Chapter 2
THE CONTROL
OF MOVEMENT

We can easily see that an animal moves its limbs in order to change its position or promote some action, and that this is accomplished by the action of muscles and tendons on bones and ligaments, but this does not tell us how the action is initiated, what force produces it, and what transmits the animal's intention from the brain to the muscles that respond, often producing an action so fast that the human eye cannot register it.

Impulses and messages are transmitted from the brain to the muscles and limbs through nerves, and these impulses are electrical, so the whole body is like a giant electronic system consisting of billions of minute cables that carry currents to and from the brain: to the brain with sensations, and from the brain for movement control.

Voluntary Nerves

These are under an animal's control; it can use them intentionally. The central nervous system (CNR), from which all messages originate through nerve fibers to limbs and organs, is in the brain and spinal cord. Forty-three pairs of trunk nerves leave this central system, and these provide vast ramifications throughout the body, vary-

11

ing in size from the thickness of a pencil to microscopically visible single fibers, myriads of which serve the fibers of the muscles.

So that there will be no leaking or diffusion of impulses from the brain to a wrong destination, each nerve fiber is surrounded by an insulating sheath containing lecithin and cholesterin, called *myelin,* and this is surrounded in turn by another fine membrane called *neurilemma.* These are separated from each other by fibrous tissue carrying tiny blood vessels to nourish them. A bundle of these insulated fibers is enclosed in a sheath of *perineurium,* and within the perineurium the fibers are divided into groups by fine partitions of a fibrous tissue known as *endoneurium,* which carries blood and lymph vessels.

Each nerve fiber originates from a single cell in the brain or spinal cord. There are millions of these, and their fibers branch out as *dendrites* in such a way that they intermingle with the dendrites of other fibers. This point of contact is known as a *synapse,* but some fibers stretch for great distances before synapsing. Others end in numerous branches serving as many muscle fibers; the branches act as a kind of plate or electrode in each of these fibers.

When stimulated, the nerve plates rapidly produce chemical changes that contract the muscle fibers, and the speed with which this takes place is quite phenomenal. The impulses travel at about a hundred feet a second, so if a nerve path from the brain to the foot of an animal is a distance of three feet (one meter), the impulses will take only one-thirtieth of a second to reach their destination. In a very small animal it might only take a thousandth of a second, and this may be part of the reason why so many small animals can react nearly instantaneously.

The largest nerve is the *sciatic* in the rear leg. It serves the most powerful locomotor muscles and must carry an immense number of impulses to countless muscle fibers. It is one of thirty-one pairs of trunk nerves originating in the spinal cord, the lower part of the CNS, which can really be considered an extension of the actual brain.

This sciatic nerve divides into two branches to supply all the muscles below the knee as well as the greater part of the skin covering the leg and foot. There is no more important nerve in the body for the control of leaping and locomotive power.

Nerve tracts are so numerous and so complicated that their full description has no place here. We need only to know how they play a part in movement. We must, however, give brief attention to two other kinds of nerves besides voluntary motor nerves.

Involuntary Nerves

Also known as *autonomic,* these continuously stimulate muscles and organs over which there is no voluntary control, such as those that keep the heart beating, the lungs functioning, the stomach digesting, and the blood vessels contracting and relaxing. These nerve fibers have no myelin sheaths, and they are much thinner than the fibers of voluntary nerves that do have sheaths. These nerves also end in involuntary muscles rather differently than the voluntary nerve fibers. They form a complicated network *between* layers of muscle, branching between the actual fibers, not into them.

Tactile or Sensory Nerves

This heading covers much more than concerns us here. We cannot deal with all sensations; only with those involved in telling an animal what its limbs are doing by sending messages from the muscles to the brain. They are called *afferent* nerves, as opposed to *efferent* nerves, which take messages from the brain.

Afferent nerves transmit a sense of touch, heat, cold, and pain. They also transmit a sense of movement and position, which is important in all forms of locomotion. It is quite a complex attribute, because it includes the sense of the exact positions of limbs and the directions in which they may be pointing. This is known as a *proprioceptive sense,* and it is actually a response to the tension and position of muscles within the body structure. The fibers send messages directly to the brain, which can then, if necessary, send impulses to the muscles to change their positions or tensions.

So, for the voluntary control of movement we have efferent nerves, which carry prompting impulses from the brain to the muscles and mediate the kind of movement desired; and afferent nerves, which return impulses to the brain, giving it an accurate picture of what is going on in those muscles. Afferent nerves serve as a checking system for the brain to judge that it is originating the right efferent messages.

Reflex Action

Sometimes action to avoid injury or death must be so fast that the time taken for a warning message by touch to reach the brain and set muscle movement in action might take a fraction of a second too long. This is avoided by shunting the afferent (to the brain) impulse at the spinal nerve to an efferent nerve serving appropriate muscles, and so cutting out the longer path to the brain and back again. In some actions this can cut out up to 60 percent of the reaction time and save a life.

Part II

MOVEMENT AND LOCOMOTION IN WATER

Chapter 3
THE EVOLUTION
OF FINS AND TAILS

Just as all life started in the waters of the earth, so, too, did the beginnings of all known patterns of movement, and every one of them is still in use there today—swimming, walking with leglike fins, wriggling or undulating, gliding, and a flying motion with batlike wings.

There have been a number of theories to account for the evolution of these forms of locomotion, for the way in which particular characteristics or anatomical forms evolved. The one most easily accepted is that in the genes of all creatures there are so many variations that every now and then a member of a species appears with something that favors its longer and easier survival, so that it can pass on its particular characteristics to more offspring in which, through the same kind of selective accident, the characteristics are further improved.

Symmetrical Form

This has been perfected in fish. As millions of years passed they became more streamlined, which aided them in increasing their speed of movement and maneuverability. But the first essential was perfect

17

symmetry—each side of the body having the same shape, form, and dimensions. This principle, once arrived at, has never been relinquished, and all creatures above a certain level in the evolutionary scale retain perfect symmetry. This certainly applies to all vertebrates.

Movement by Undulation

The earliest vertebrate method of progression through water was the undulating snakelike movement by which the creation of a muscular wave motion down the body produces back pressure against the water and forces the animal along. The first pre-vertebrates, like the lancelet and amphioxus, had this undulating motion, and animals such as balinoglossus must have had it, too. It is seen in its most perfect form in sea snakes, which, after evolving into completely land-bound animals, returned to the sea once more, perhaps to find new sources of food.

These snakes have evolved a slightly flattened tail, but have not reverted to the development of fins. Almost the same form of locomotion can be seen in lampreys, hagfish, and eels. Eels may have reverted back to some extent, like snakes, but they do demonstrate the basic fish movements. This wave motion is the same to a greater or lesser degree in most fish, especially the fast swimmers. Only armor-plated fish and those using electrical currents for orientation

4. *The eel propels itself by an undulating body movement. The rear end of its body is somewhat flattened to increase the force it can apply to the water.*

keep their bodies rigid. Fins seldom play any part in locomotion; they are stabilizers and steering organs only.

This undulating movement used to progress through water by creatures with symmetrical shape has favored the flattening of the rear end of a body to produce a greater thrust, and throughout the long history of fish, this flattening has assumed many different vertical shapes and dimensions, becoming what we call the *caudal fin* or tail.

The shapes of fish tails are not capricious; each is a design for maximum efficiency for the form of fish using it. Fast swimmers will naturally not have the same shape of tail as fish that merely hover around reefs or in crevices. Similarly, fish with long bodies will need different-shaped tails from those that are short and chunky, because stability of posture is involved, and to some extent the tail assists a fish to remain in one position as well as being an aid to the undulation of the body in its task of moving the fish forward. It is also a steering oar.

True Tails

The first form of true tail may have been *diphycercal,* although there is not complete agreement on this. This form is still seen in lungfish and coelocanths (see Figure 6). It is a straight extension of the body, perfectly symmetrical, and with the vertebrae extending right to its tip.

The next form to become widely adopted may have been *heterocercal,* and this is still seen today in most sharks. The vertebrae turn upward at the root of the tail, and most of the actual tail structure is below this (see Figure 7). It is different from most bony fish, but nevertheless is a very effective steering organ.

Many modifications of these shapes were experimented with throughout fish history, some the exact reverse of the present heterocercal form; but the shape finally adopted by most fish is vertically symmetrical with two lobes, an upper and a lower. This shape has been found in 190-million-year-old fossils.

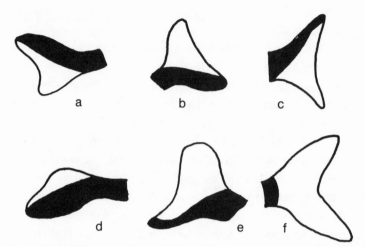

5. *In the development of the fish tail, many forms have evolved. In this drawing the black part shows the position of the vertebrae.* a *is the form adopted by most sharks, but together with* e *and* d *it was also used by a great many primitive fish.* b *was used by some specialized sharks,* c *by early bony fish, and* f *is the pattern used by modern bony fish* (see also Figure 7).

6. Left, *a typical diphycercal tail. It is on a coelocanth, a very primitive fish that has survived in its present form for millions of years.* Right, *the tail of a fast-swimming fish, a sailfish* (Istiophorus spp.).

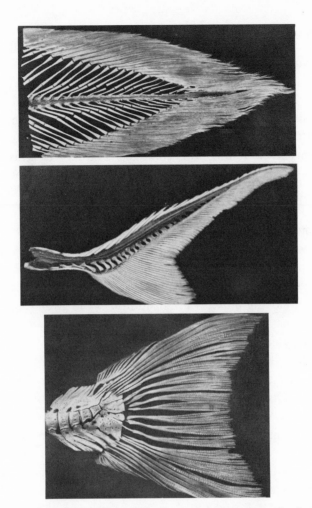

7. Top, *the skeleton of a diphycercal tail;* center, *a heterocercal tail skeleton as found in most sharks;* bottom, *the tail skeleton of a modern teleost (bony) fish tail.*

Because so many of the earliest fish were armor-plated, we can assume that their body movement was much more restricted than is the case with the majority of modern fish, and the tail must therefore have played a greater part in actual forward movement than it may do now, as well as in maneuvering. At the same time there was poor development of or even absence of paired fins, so agility must have also been very limited and almost entirely dependent on the tail.

Functional Fins

Active fish have perfected their balance and streamlined effect by having their greatest body diameter a little ahead of the halfway mark. Although pairs of fins occupy positions on the body where they ultimately were able to become the front legs or arms (*pectoral fins*) and hind legs (*pelvic fins*) of land vertebrates, there are others that remain single and central to the body axis. These are *dorsal, anal,* and *caudal,* the last being the tail.

Fins probably began as flaps or spines, most probably the latter, and although some of them may have developed after tails, they certainly appeared very early in fish history. Each of the pectoral and pelvic fins is attached to a girdle of bone or cartilage within the body, and the fin-moving muscles originate from these girdles.

Medial fins may well have been developing very soon after tails, because they can be seen in fossils up to 385 million years old, and some hydrofoillike fins were present in early sharklike fish up to 380 million years ago. These have been discarded since then, and the evidence points to tails, fins, and a number of other fish characteristics having all evolved within a fairly short time span.

Their continued development and improvement were related to the capture of prey, or escape from predators, and so in those fish that did not choose to hide, use camouflage, or adopt a protective environment, the entire trend was toward greater speed and powers of maneuver. This led to the present forms, some of which are capable of bursts of speed that will even carry them far into the air.

Vertebrates that after eons of time devoted to living on land have returned to the sea, such as porpoises, whales, seals, and so on have had to redevelop tails and fins (flippers), and these are described in Chapter 5.

Chapter 4

FISH: THEIR SWIMMING ACTION AND SPEEDS

Those fish described in Chapter 3 are by no means the only success-ful forms. There are flatfish that live on the sea bottom, fish that roam the open seas, and others that have developed their pectoral fins into fleshy limbs for walking and climbing. These last are dealt with more appropriately in Chapter 7.

Caudal Propulsion

Gravity exerts almost no force on fish, so all their strength can be used for propulsion alone. It also permits the maximum effectiveness of their paired fins in body control, rotation, and braking. There are three main kinds of *caudal propulsion,* which were described in Chapter 3 as swimming action. One uses the tail and a very small part of the adjacent body, obvious in some of the rigid-bodied and armored fish. In the second at least half the body is flexed, as in the active swimmers—herring, mackerel, salmon, et cetera—and in the third almost the entire body length is used in an undulating action. This is seen in eels.

Movement through water appears to be almost effortless for most fish because of the negligible effects of gravity. Their shapes have evolved to produce the least possible resistance to water flow. Resistance is caused by eddies, and only body shape can reduce these to a minimum. It is so important to avoid making eddies down the sides of the body that many species of fast-swimming fish, such as the herring, have even evolved vertical folds of transparent skin beside their eyes to prevent eddies being created by the slight bulge of the eyes.

For a long time it was thought that fish move through the water by a combined triple action of flipping their tails, undulating their bodies, and waving their fins. But healthy fish can swim almost as well without their fins and tails as they can with them unless they are among the few rigid-bodied forms already mentioned. It is more difficult to maintain a static position without these organs, however.

Muscle Power

The swimming speeds of fish, and even of marine mammals, are so much greater than is theoretically possible for their known muscle power that even with the elimination of gravity pull, eddies, and water resistance there must also be an unusual economy of energy and use of food possible to fish that is not enjoyed by land animals.

Although in most fish their fins only stabilize the vertical and sideways motions, their propelling force through body undulation is by a very interesting action. The muscle segments on one side of a part of the body contract while those on the opposite side relax, the process being continuously reversed from side to side. This passes an undulating motion down the entire length of the body from head to tail with a wave speed that is greater than the swimming speed, producing thrust on each side alternately, the wave growing larger as it approaches the tail.

Eddies produced *behind* a swimming fish help to create a whirling wake or vortex, and this adds to forward thrust. Some fish can use ready-made eddies to help them keep their position and save energy. They do this by hovering behind a rock or in a gully when facing a

8. *Fish move through the contraction of muscle segments on one side or part of the body while those on the opposite side relax.*

current, or by swimming in such a position behind other fish that they are drawn along by the eddies created by fish ahead of them. This device is used by fish swimming in schools.

Some fins are quite specific in their stabilizing and steering function. The dorsal, pelvic, and pectoral fins prevent rolling and yawing in much the same way as stabilizers built into modern oceangoing ships. The pectoral and anal fins are used also for maneuvering and braking. However, in some very fast fish, the dorsal and anal fins are laid back against the body while they are swimming, and the pectorals alone are used for turning.

The shape of a tail is important in aiding this steering and stabilizing action, and different shapes give different degrees of control as well as impetus; but together with body shape they act mostly to give lift and eddy pressure behind for peak performance. In bony fish, the symmetrical tail produces more forward thrust, whereas in sharks, the larger upper lobe of the tail produces an upward as well as a forward thrust. In those fish that hover motionless in one spot for a time, probably all the fins are used to make this possible.

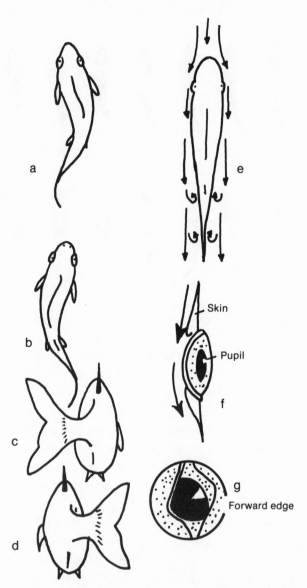

Skin

Pupil

Forward edge

9. a *and* b *show the undulating movement that passes along a fish's body as it produces the side-to-side thrust that propels it, and* c *and* d *show the same action from behind.* e. *The shape of a fish's body creates turbulence mainly where it will add to forward thrust. To ensure that no minor turbulence is created elsewhere by projecting tissue, some fast-swimming fish have special skin folds to prevent this developing from the bulge of the eye. This is shown in* f *and* g.

10. *The most effortless motion in a fish is possible only when body shape permits an eddy-free laminar flow of water over it until it reaches the last part of the tapered body.*

Swimming Speeds

Observations carried out on fish size and swimming speed by Dr. T. Yau-tsu at the California Institute of Technology, Howard R. Kelly of the Naval Ordinance Test Station at China Lake, California, and Glen Bowles of the Pasadena office of the same station, produced some interesting results. The tests were done on trout.

Fish length	Tail-beat frequency	Speed of movement
1.5 inches	24 per second	26.4 inches per second
11.0 inches	16 per second	114.0 inches per second

Some of the measured speeds of other fish have proved to be very impressive compared with those of land animals and man-made machines, especially when considering that water is 800 times denser than air. The speed of a swordfish, said to be 60 miles per hour, is phenomenal. So are the speeds of bluefin tuna (44 mph), bonito (50 mph), wahoo (40 mph), salmon (25 mph), and mackerel (20 mph). But perhaps such speeds are less surprising when two-fifths of the body volume consists of swimming muscle, three-fourths in tuna. Some of these speeds may be exaggerated, because another estimate has placed the speed of tuna nearer to 30 miles per hour. However, much always depends on the species being observed and the size of the fish.

The top speed of a fish can be kept up for only a short time. Really high speeds are possible sometimes for a few seconds, but the cruising speed of any fish can always be sustained for a long period. Herrings are, however, one group that can keep up high speed relative to body length, as can tunny and barracuda, which have a very high ratio of power to body weight.

Although the majority of fish move in the way described, there are, as in everything nature develops, some exceptions. Perhaps the commonest of those is the sea horse, which swims upright, with the movement of its dorsal fin alone. Fish that lie on the bottom, especially skates and rays, and those that have become flattened as a result of adopting this habit late in their history, swim in an entirely different manner.

Flatfish

Rays undulate their enlarged lateral fins to propel themselves, but flattened teleosts such as halibut and flounder undulate their bodies in

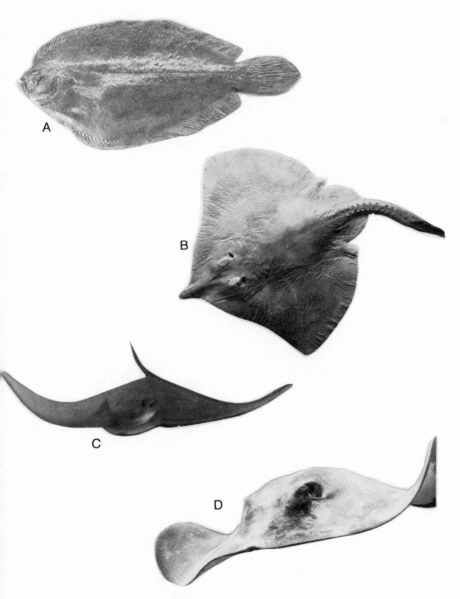

11. *Flatfish take two forms: the bony fish, which lie on one side, one of their eyes migrating around to the other side; and the skates and rays. A is a sole, B a skate, and C and D are rays. The bull-nosed or cow-nosed ray (Rhinoptera bonasi) at the left flaps its winglike pectoral fins to swim, and the so-called Captain Cook ray at the right undulates them.*

a vertical direction just like other bony fish. The movement merely appears to be different because they have adapted to lying on their sides. They can make a quick getaway by forcing a jet of water through the gill on the underside of the body.

An ancient fish found in Ohio and Germany in fossil form was something like a modern batfish in appearance, but it has also been likened to a somewhat armored ray, so this pattern of swimming is also very ancient.

Chapter 5

MAMMALS RETURN TO THE SEA

Whatever the reasons well-established land animals had for returning to an ocean life, the need for a new or improved food supply must have been at least one of them, because so many of these animals are highly carnivorous. Almost the only feature of land living retained by most of them is their need to breathe air, and yet it can hardly have been more than 40 million years since they began to develop toward their present form and way of life, because modern mammals as a whole have had a history of only approximately 50 million years.

In spite of this relatively short period of development, marine mammals are as perfectly suited to their environment as the most highly evolved fish. In many ways they are similar to fish in their mechanics of locomotion, and yet it is obvious they have not returned to exactly the same pattern; merely a similar one. There are four main groups of purely marine mammals. They are:

1. Whales, porpoises, dolphins
2. Seals, sea lions, walruses, et cetera
3. Manatees and dugongs
4. Sea otters

Whales (Cetacea)

Porpoises and dolphins are included among the whale group; they also are true whales. However, there are different swimming habits found within the group. In some porpoises and dolphins, propulsion is either by flexion of the whole body, as in sharks and some bony fish, or by action of the tail alone. Whales do not have vertical tails or caudal fins, but instead have horizontal *flukes* (as a tail), so their propulsion is based on an up-and-down and curving movement rather than a lateral one like fish. This is accompanied by an up-and-down undulation of the body.

The flukes have no bony support apart from the end of the spine; they are merely horizontal expansions of skin and fibrous tissue stiffened by a layer of strong ligamentous fibers from the base to the tips, and moved up and down by great trunk muscles, the tendons of

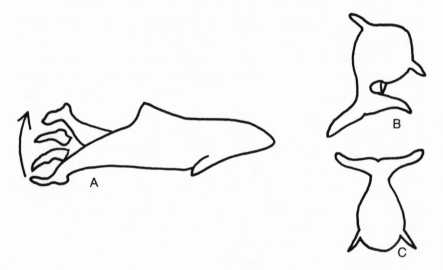

12. The flukes (tails) of whales (including dolphins) operate by an up-and-down motion instead of the sideways movement used by fish. This is shown at left (A). B and C show two positions adopted by dolphins to ride the bow waves of ships, by which they are then propelled without effort. The upper of the two is the commoner posture, the body accepting the thrust, and the tail used to retain elevation.

13. *The whale's flukes are supported by no bone structure except the spinal vertebrae shown here.*

which are attached to the end of the spine. In cetaceans, the muscles of the back, having to work against the action of gravity, little though this is in water, are the most powerful in the body, so the main power stroke is the upstroke. The downstroke merely serves to return the tail to the down position.

The dorsal fin has much the same structure as the tail. It has neither bone nor muscle in it, but is an extension of skin and fibrous tissue from the back, strengthened by strong ligamentous material. The blue whale (*Balaenoptera musculus*) and sperm whale (*Physeter macrocephalus*) have negligible dorsal fins. Dolphins have dorsal fins in different positions and of different sizes, according to the species.

The forelimbs of land mammals have considerable freedom of movement in all their joints, but the flipper limbs of whales, although they have the same basic structure, are modified to suit the needs of locomotion in water. The humerus is short, the ulnar and radius flattened, the wrist bones mosaiclike with a larger number of digital bones (see Figure 14), acting as the foundation of a fingerless fin. Movement is confined to the shoulders, the flippers controlling direction of movement and braking, but not contributing to propulsion.

In their embryos, the whale flipper and the human arm are identical from the beginning of their development to a certain point, and it is not until they are past this point that they begin to differentiate. So the flippers actually begin as limbs like our arms.

14. *The probable pattern of development of the tail* (left) *and the fins* (right) *of whales: The inset shows the hidden bones of the present form of flipper.*

There is no external trace of a hind limb in adult whales, although some do have an internal vestige of this called a *chevron* bone, and occasionally a remnant of a thigh bone is found in some whalebone whales. In some species the chevron bone is slender and about twelve inches long, buried in a mass of muscle, and in some of them a small bone projects from its side. The longer bone is a remnant of a pelvis, and the smaller bone, which may not be more than an inch in length, is a vestigial femur. In one or two whales a smaller vestige of a tibia is also found attached to the femur.

Whale body musculature is similar to that of fish in spite of great size differences. Such bulk of muscle in an element that exerts minimal gravity force should give these animals great speed, but other factors are naturally involved—blood circulation, water resistance to body shape, and body flexibility. Their speeds are not equal to those of the fastest bony fish.

The blue whale (*Balaenoptera musculus*) has 40 percent of its body weight in muscle, against 17 percent in bony skeleton. Finback (*Balaenoptera physalus*) and sei (*Balaenoptera borealis*) whales have 45 percent and 54 percent of their body weights, respectively, in muscle. Porpoises have similar proportions. The reason for such lightness of bone structure is that these animals do not have to support their weight; this is done by the water, and the skeleton only anchors the muscles.

Most whales do not swim particularly fast. Many of them cruise at about 5 miles per hour, while the remainder range between 2 and 23 mph. A sprinting speed on the surface has been registered on one occasion as 40 mph, but this must be rare. Dolphins can maintain 23 mph for quite a time, and speeds of 34 to 36 mph have been measured when they are riding the bow waves of destroyers, but this is hardly swimming speed, and they are probably enjoying a kind of toboggan sport.

The actual swimming movements of a dolphin are the opposite to those of fish. The oscillations of the body are vertical, and the horizontally held flukes move up and down also, the fins and flippers being used only as stabilizers. This kind of movement seems very efficient, however, for the dolphin can maintain a speed of 23 mph with two beats of its tail a second. The tail can move slightly laterally in some species, but this is only contributing to steering, not to propulsion. As the tail moves down, the flukes curl up, and as the tail moves up, the flukes curl down.

The flow of water along a dolphin's body is laminar. If it were not, the animal would need about seven times the amount of muscle it does have. Seals, on the other hand, create a great deal of turbulence, so they must use more power to swim at a given speed than the dolphin needs. The longer the body of a whale, the greater the turbulence, and the farther back the maximum girth, the more the disturbance. All this plays a part in controlling the speed at which they can swim.

Considerable attention has been given to the swimming action of dolphins. Their size and willingness to work with man in captivity makes them ideal subjects. It has been found that body-surface drag is almost absent in them. This has been demonstrated with the use of dyes, suspended particles in water, and high-speed movie cameras taking up to four hundred pictures a second. Around a dolphin's nose there is very little blood, and therefore no appreciable heat given off to the surrounding water to create turbulence. Toward the tail, however, there is a great vascular circulation with consequent heat transference to the water, and this does create turbulence to help propel them from behind.

Seals (Pinnipedia)

Seals are not so entirely sea-bound as whales, but they are very clumsy on land, and only come ashore to bask or breed. Locomotion on land is labored because their hind limbs cannot be brought forward to support the body, and walking consists of caterpillar movements in which the forelimbs are used to raise the chest and hitch the animal along.

The common seal (Phoca vitulina) has short, stout fore flippers, with little more than the hand projecting from the body surface. These are not used for propulsion, but are held against the surface of the body as the animal undulates its body from side to side, its outstretched hind limbs acting like the flukes of whales.

The hind limbs of the sea leopard or leopard seal (Hydrurga leptonyx) are fused together so that they are like a tail; they cannot be

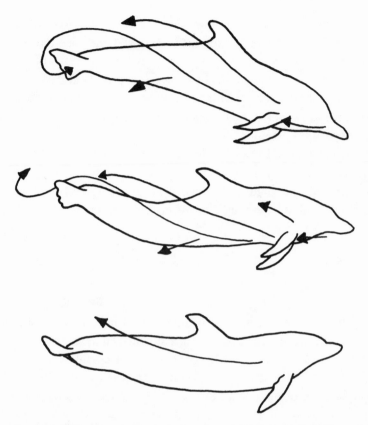

15. *Some of the directions of laminar flow over a dolphin's body as the action of the tail flukes accelerates water obliquely over the body and past the faired edge of the back behind the dorsal fin so that the vortex is washed away. When the animal has reached its maximum velocity and has exhausted its power stroke, the tail flukes are held in a glide position parallel with the line of motion, and they then offer very little resistance to the water. Then the lower muscles pull the tail downward, aided by the hydrofoil cross-section of the flukes, which begin to curl upward and spill water sideways instead of accelerating it to the rear. This raises the front part of the body.*

turned forward like those of some other seals, particularly the sea lion (*Zalophus spp.*) and the fur seal (*Arctocephalus spp.*), in which the hind flippers can even be turned forward independently of each other.

The digits in a seal's forelimb diminish in length from the first to the fifth, but in the hind flipper the first and fifth are the longest, those in between being shorter. Sea lions and fur seals (Otariidae) have much longer flippers than true seals, and on land they are more mobile, the hind limbs having retained a more normal posture, and being able to support the hind end of the body. In these animals, the fore flippers are also used in swimming.

Most seals have a side-to-side movement when swimming. As the body moves left, the right rear flipper comes into play and vice versa, but some seals are able to undulate their bodies up and down as well as from side to side. Always, however, there seems to be a turbulent wake.

Sirenians

The manatees and dugongs, or sea cows, are like seals in having transformed their forelimbs into flippers; but like whales, they have laterally expanded tails and have discarded their rear limbs. The sirenian tail has no notch and is somewhat diphycercal. The modifications of the flippers are not so great as in whales, and there is still much freedom of movement in the wrists, elbows, and fingers.

Because these animals are wholly herbivorous, they are leisurely swimmers, lingering and lying in seaweed beds. They never come on land, so in this respect they are again like whales. Even their young are born submerged, just as baby whales are.

Sea Otters

Although these mammals (*Enhydra lutris*) have true legs, they seldom come on land, where they are much clumsier than their freshwater relatives. They have evolved from sea visitors to almost completely water-bound animals, using their thick tails and sinuous bodies for swimming; but any similarity to other sea mammals ends there.

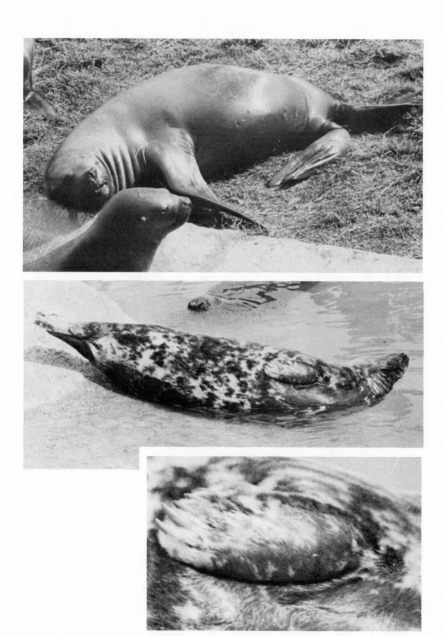

16. *Sea lions and fur seals have much longer flippers than common seals. In the top picture these long flippers are obvious, as is the ability of the hind limbs to turn forward for walking. Below, the leopard seal, a fast swimmer, can be seen to have very short forelimbs with clearly demarcated fingers (see close-up).*

Other Mammals

The monotreme platypus (*Ornithorhynchus anatinus*), although not a marine mammal, is almost wholly aquatic. Its four feet are fully webbed between all five digits, and it uses these as efficient paddles, while its flattened tail acts as a steering organ. Its constant search for food, of which it requires great quantities to compensate for heat loss to the water, keeps it away from its burrow and searching the riverbed for long periods.

The polar bear (*Thalarctos maritimus*) must be mentioned for its strange swimming pattern. It is a powerful swimmer and enters arctic water quite readily to catch fish. Viewed from below, it can be seen to use only its great forelegs for paddling, allowing its hind legs to trail curled up beneath its rump.

Chapter 6
SWIMMING AND DIVING BIRDS

Birds that have taken to swimming and diving, either in the ocean or fresh water, have done so in relation to food gathering. Those that have a fish diet either dive straight onto their prey or chase it under water, and some of these underwater swimmers can attain surprising speeds. For instance, the gentoo penguin (*Pygoscelis papua*) has been timed swimming under water at about 22 mph.

Almost all swimming birds have webbed feet, and many also use their wings for sculling. Those that dive skillfully are not usually good fliers, because if the wings are used for swimming they must be shaped to create the least turbulence under water. This is probably not the same as avoiding turbulence in the air. The good divers usually have small, thin, but muscular wings.

Sculling under Water

Besides penguins, birds that chase their prey under water by paddling with their wings include petrels, shearwaters, cormorants, auks, and guillemots. The petrels and shearwaters are also excellent fliers, covering immense migratory distances each year by using air currents that enable them to conserve energy. This is described fully in Chapter 12.

There are some interesting adaptations to the sculling habit, and not all birds that use their wings for this purpose do so under water. The flightless steamer duck (*Tachyeres brachypterus*) of Patagonia uses its wings for swimming on the surface of the water like true oars or paddles.

Even more unusual behavior is seen in the diving petrel (*Pelecanoides urinatrix*). It not only uses its wings as paddles under water, but leaves the water in full flight, carrying on its wing motion right into the air. Other petrels, like the shearwaters (*Puffinus griseus,* et cetera) and the albatross (*Diomedea spp.*), run on the water surface to take off, gaining speed in this way before lifting into the wind.

Perhaps the best scullers are the penguins. All species of penguins have long since sacrificed flight for underwater hunting, using their wings, now evolved into flippers, as paddles. They either beat them simultaneously or alternately. One may act as a brake while the other exerts a forward force, and this produces extreme maneuvering ability. The speeds these birds attain permit them to leap from the water to considerable heights to get onto ice floes or rock shelves, and a six-foot leap is no obstacle to them. They can, in fact, swim just as fast as seals.

The contour of a penguin's wing is very much like the pectoral fin of a shark, and it functions in much the same way as far as stabilizing the bird is concerned. The wrist and elbow have become rigid so that all movement is from the shoulder, and in many species the wing has become almost knifelike so that it is ideal for cutting through the water. The webbed feet play only a secondary part in swimming under water, although they are used alone sometimes on the surface as they paddle between dives.

As clumsy on land as these adaptations make penguins, some species walk great distances from the open sea to their nests on the ice or land, and often at a considerable pace.

17. *Penguin wings, used solely as flippers, are well illustrated in this king penguin* (Aptenodytes patagonica), *as is the streamlined body shape. Found in the Antarctic, this is the second-largest penguin species, standing 3 feet high.*

Swimming Feet

No living or extinct bird appears to have more than four toes on each foot; some have three and a few have only two. The fourth toe always points backward, and even the archaeopteryx had this pattern millions of years ago. The slenderness of bird toes would render them quite unsuitable for swimming, and this had to be overcome by in-

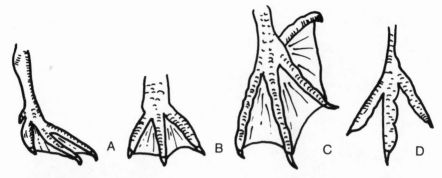

18. *Most swimming birds have their three forward toes webbed, as in the swan (A) and penguin (B). Only the pelicans and cormorants have all four toes joined by webs (C). Coots, phalaropes, and grebes have skin flaps on their toes (D), which, though giving less power than full webs, are still very effective power units for swimming, and at the same time act like snowshoes on mud.*

creasing the surface area that could be used to put pressure on the water. This has been done in two ways: by joining the toes with a flexible web of skin in most species, and by developing lobes of skin on each toe in a few others. (See Figure 18.)

Only one family of birds has all four toes united with a web, the *pelecaniformes;* all the rest merely have three. As the foot is brought forward, ready for a swimming stroke, it folds tight to present as little resistant surface to the water as possible, and then it opens wide as the back-pressing stroke begins. In birds such as loons and grebes, greater driving power is added to the stroke by the femur's being short and stocky.

A few of the birds with webbed feet are flamingos, pelicans, and all other seabirds; ducks, geese, and swans. Coots (*Fulica spp.*) have broad lobes of skin along the edges of each toe. These aid not only in swimming, but for walking on mud like a snowshoe. Terns and sea swallows have their webs scalloped, but there is no obvious reason for this.

To improve their swimming performance, ducks, auks, guillemots, puffins, divers, and loons all have their legs set well back on the body. This is a disadvantage for walking on land, and most of these birds are consequently poor walkers. In fact, the majority of swimming birds are clumsy on land. Grebes cannot even take flight on land; they must be able to run on the surface of the water.

Divers and loons (*gaviiformes*) use their webbed feet only for swimming under water. Divers (*Gavia spp.*), like grebes, can only walk on land with difficulty, and they are really poor fliers as well.

Diving Birds

The most spectacular divers don't necessarily enter the water at the end of a dive. The frigate bird (*Fregata spp.*) is an example of this. It may have a seven-foot wingspan for only a three-and-a-half-pound body weight, so although it is a poor walker and swimmer, it is a marvelous flier. It will dive from a great height and capture surface-swimming fish without entering the water at all.

Gannets (*Morus spp.* and *Sula spp.*), however, will plunge from

19. Tropic birds (Phaëthon spp.) *are both skilled fliers and expert fishers, their wide wingspan giving them superb control.*

heights up to 100 feet in their dives, and may go almost as deep below the surface. Loons have even been found to reach depths up to 240 feet or more in a dive. The azure kingfisher (*Alcyone azurea*), although a relatively tiny bird, dives from any height up to 30 feet to catch its small prey, so it is obvious that many of these diving birds enter the water very much like projectiles.

It is interesting how the many seabirds have such different skills, and to such varying degrees. Auks, guillemots, and puffins are great divers and swimmers, but gulls never dive, although they are good walkers and swimmers. Terns, by contrast, are bad walkers but excellent fliers and divers. Some pelicans have a ten-foot wingspan and are considered to be spectacular divers, but really only one species, the brown pelican (*Pelican occidentalis*), does this.

Many species of ducks are good divers, but only from a surface swimming position.

Divers and grebes add to their diving efficiency in a surprising way. They are able to expel air from their bodies by emptying the cavities, or sacs, that supplement their lungs, and to expel the air trapped in their feathers. This reduces their buoyancy and permits them to go deeper. On surfacing they recharge their cavities with air via their lungs. There may be other birds that do this, but it is so far only obvious in these species.

Part III

THE DEMANDS
OF MOVING FROM
WATER TO LAND

Chapter 7
THE EVOLUTION
OF TERRESTRIAL LIMBS

Walking fish, mentioned in Chapter 4, might seem the obvious ancestral forms suitable for amphibian development. Walking fish certainly appeared very early in fish history, but as important as legs or feet are, the possession of lungs might be even more essential, and the two did not always evolve together. Many fish developed lungs in great drought periods experienced by the world three to four hundred million years ago, and some of their descendants are still with us. Walking fish, however, have not all developed lungs.

Walking Fins

The mudskipper (*Periophthalmos spp.*) and the climbing perch (*Anabas testudineus*) can remain out of water for long periods. The mudskipper (Figure 20) prefers to be on damp ground, and if possible have its tail in water to absorb oxygen through its skin, but it can remain completely away from water for a short time. The climbing perch only climbs trees in wet weather, when it, too, can absorb oxygen in water through its skin. Neither of these groups have true lungs, and the climbing perch does not even have a gas bladder.

Another fish that supports its body on its pectoral fins, like the

20. *The mudskipper* (Periophthalmos spp.) *likes to get some of its oxygen by keeping its tail in water, but it can in fact do without water for some time.*

mudskipper and the climbing perch, is the bichir (*Polypterus congicus*) of Africa. There are also a number of angler fish that walk on limblike fins on the ocean bottom and in banks of weed (see Figure 21), but these are not necessarily related to any amphibian ancestors, which were undoubtedly freshwater species.

Lungfish still living in South America, Africa, and Australia are probably the closest to the earliest amphibian ancestors, especially since some of these lungfish also walk on their fins. But they are a group on the road to extinction, and probably not much like the true ancestors except that they have evolved similar habits. One ancient fish (*Cephalaspis*), a primitive jawless species whose fossils have been found in Devonian strata (about 350 million years ago), had bones in its fins that correspond closely to the limb bones of amphib-

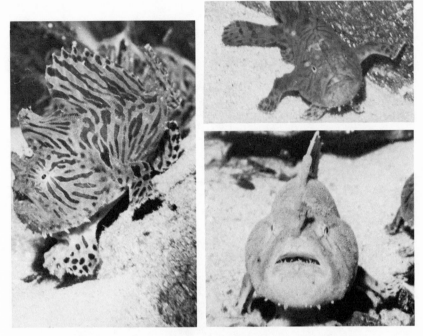

21. A number of angler fish walk stolidly along the ocean bottom or in banks of weed on leglike fins, as shown here in specimens of Antennarius striatus.

ians, reptiles, and mammals. At this time the first amphibians were appearing, so this fish may be more typical of primitive amphibians than anything surviving today.

The earliest amphibians spent a great deal of their time in water, but sometime between 300 and 400 million years ago, a few of them began to move more freely onto land with the four primitive feet they had developed from fins. Why they did this is not clear, because being carnivorous, their food was still predominantly in the fresh waters. The only plausible explanation seems to be that they had to adapt in this way as waters dried up in many parts of the world and they were compelled to move around in search of more water.

They may then have preyed on each other and on the abundant insect life already on land. There were certainly long periods of great drought around 350 million years ago that would account for this theory.

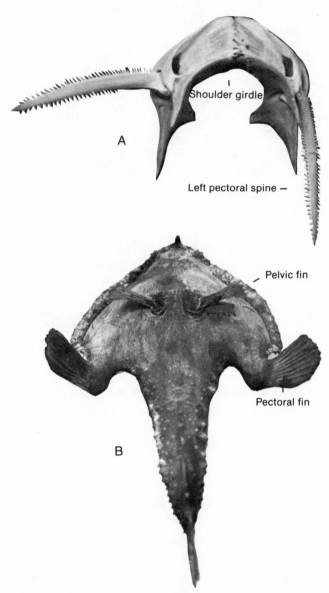

22. A *shows the powerful shoulder girdles and extended front rays of the pectoral fins of* Doras muricus, *an armored catfish that can travel overland for considerable distances. These fish do not breathe air but keep water in their closed gill chambers.* B *is a deep-sea batfish* (Halieutaea brevicauda), *which can walk out of water for hours with no apparent discomfort.*

Amphibians Choose Their Forms

Quite early in their history, amphibians formed into two groups. From one evolved the salamanders (*urodeles*) and the wormlike *apoda,* and from the other the frogs and toads (*anura*) derived. The full history is very complex, and no doubt the transition from fleshy fins to well-formed legs was a slow and circuitous one.

The locomotion of amphibians on land is related to their forms as just described for the two ancestral groups. Some have retained their aquatic pattern of locomotion and move very much like eels. Even salamanders have a certain amount of this eellike movement, in spite of having well-formed legs. Present-day amphibians, unlike reptiles and most mammals, have only four toes or less on each front foot (or hand).

Frogs and some toads use their powerful hind legs for leaping, and so effective are these that some frogs can complete a leap of several times their own length in a twentieth of a second. The rest of the toads walk in a four-legged manner. Frogs and toads also use their rear legs for swimming. Newts walk on their four legs, and they even

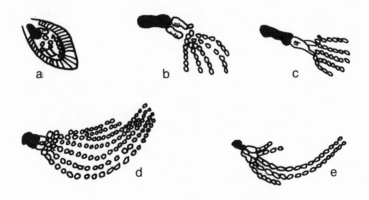

23. *In this diagram there is a reconstruction of* a, *an ancestral footlike fin;* b, *a primitive reptilian foot;* c, *a primitive mammalian foot;* d, *the foot or flipper of an early ichthyosaur; and* e, *the flipper of a modern whale.*

do this on the mud bottom under water, although they swim like fish, with their legs pressed to their sides.

All amphibians have sacrificed their speed and agility in water, and most have not redeveloped it to any extent on land. Urodele limbs do not even support the body when it is at rest. The body remains in contact with the ground, and many retain an eellike undulating pattern of movement, using the front legs to steer the body. They actually "swim" over the ground, the positions of their limbs apparently having evolved in relation to this kind of movement.

Chapter 8
REPTILES GO FOUR WAYS

The Importance of Eggshell

The ancestors of reptiles, which were some primitive forms of amphibians, are less difficult to imagine than the ancestors of amphibians themselves. Once a hard shell that would prevent the contents of an egg from dehydrating had been developed, there was no reason for animals to return to water to breed, so they could move further away from it. The land was then truly on the way to being fully conquered.

The reptiles developed this watertight egg, and so were able to populate the earth in vast numbers, but by 100 million years ago their numbers were reducing rapidly as populations of the more adaptable mammals increased and competed with them for the available space and food. However, some reptiles also improved their adaptability. This can be seen in lizards that, as we know them now, may have no more than 150 million years of history, even though there are more than two thousand species.

Most reptiles retained the short legs of their amphibian ancestors, but they developed more powerful muscles and much greater walking ability. Later they adopted several patterns of locomotion, some using equal-sized limbs, others developing long hind legs and very short forelegs. Some developed flight and were the ancestors of the entire avian group (see Chapter 11), a number returned to the sea, a few learned to glide, and one great group, the snakes and snake-lizards, sacrificed their legs for a slithering or fishlike form of loco-motion useful for getting into less accessible places.

Some reptiles, whether they have legs or not, are able to attain great speed in relation to their body size, with a phenomenal power of acceleration and ability to change direction. Many have longer and more powerful hind limbs than forelimbs, and these hind limbs pro-vide their main motive power. Some run on their hind legs alone.

There is a tilting forward of the body in these animals, but this is balanced by a powerful tail in which are rooted the muscles that move the legs. Their legs are also placed closer toward the middle of the body and thus support the weight of the body more centrally. The feet point in a more forward direction, and the central toes, which are the longest, are used for traction.

Such lizards not only have much less-developed forelegs, but the fingers of these are often degenerate as well, sometimes almost non-existent. Many of the now extinct giant reptiles also ran on their hind legs only.

A few reptiles still show movement reminiscent of fish, even though they have legs. Alligators and crocodiles, except when they are in a hurry, move this way even while using their legs. Early reptiles that retained their legs had five digits on each hand and foot, and this seems to be an advancement since the amphibians have only four digits on each front foot. Some reptiles later gave up one of the digits on each hind foot.

A Return to the Water

Lizard feet are also more easily swung into position than those of amphibians. This is a modern development, because the strange gait of tortoises is considered to be like that used by the earlier reptiles.

Many ancient forms of reptiles returned to the sea, redeveloping their feet into fins and their end vertebrae into swimming tails. These are now all extinct. The turtles have survived, but instead of trying to adapt to the high speeds of other reptiles and marine inhabitants, they retained their legs as paddles and their carapaces for protection.

The relatively modern species of reptiles we call *marine lizards* are not adapted to a true marine life. They enter and leave water, and can remain submerged for considerable periods, but they have retained the limbs and movements of land lizards, using their tails and sinuous bodies to swim with an undulating motion. In the Nile monitor (*Varanus niloticus*) and the Malay monitor (*Varanus salvator*), the tail has become flattened vertically, and a finlike crest is present along the back. Both of these features are adaptations for aquatic life, but the animals are still largely terrestrial.

A number of aquatic lizards, like land lizards, are extremely fast and agile when running, often climbing trees with considerable speed. Other *varanid* lizards that never see bodies of water, even those confined to semidesert regions, do this too. In fact, they have been known to run up a man when startled in a place where they are not within reach of any other vertical object to climb.

Several species of desert-dwelling lizards, mostly iguanas and geckos, have developed fringes of scales on their toes, which then act like snowshoes to prevent them from sinking into soft sand as they run.

Crocodiles and alligators are of very ancient origin, and their methods of locomotion can be divided into three patterns. One is a fishlike undulation, with the feet used as levers against the ground, and this may be related to the front legs' being shorter than the rear. This motion is much the same as their movement in water as far as the body undulation is concerned.

A second method is a slow, deliberate walk, still dragging the body along the ground; and the third method is a surprisingly fast run, with the body raised well above the ground on straight legs. The tail is flattened, and this is their main aid to swimming, apart from body movement.

The Legless Ones

Snakes evolved from true lizards not more than 100 million years ago. They are not descended from legless lizards, but from varanid-type lizards. Their perfection of fishlike movement became possible with the acquisition of a freely moving rib system, more vertebrae (up to four hundred), and large, transverse, horny scales on the underside to grip the surface over which they travel. Such a grip is not possible, however, unless the ground is rough. The scales move forward in steady succession, drawing the body along with them.

In addition to gripping the ground with these scales, those snakes that undulate their bodies use the loops thus formed to create a back pressure against the ground, and this provides very considerable additional leverage. Although most snakes use their ventral scales and muscles as just described, burrowing snakes (and lizards) use their dorsal muscles as well. Most boas and vipers use their ventral scales only, without undulating their bodies from side to side; instead, they send waves of muscle contractions from head to tail, curving their bodies only to gain striking distance. Boas and pythons also have tiny spurs that mark the former positions of the hind legs sacrificed by their ancestors.

24. *Although modern snakes are not descended from legless lizards, like this* Siaphos equalis *shown here, a number of lizards have sacrificed their legs even more than this species, which has adopted a snakelike movement rendering its legs quite useless. The legs are in the process of complete degeneration.*

Many snakes, perhaps most, are excellent swimmers, and many are also agile tree climbers. Some even live in trees. The best swimmers, the sea snakes, never come on land at all except to have their young, although they may rest on reefs. Except for one Asian species (*Laticauda colubrina*), they have lost the power to move easily on land, since the ventral scales used by land snakes are so small in sea snakes as to be virtually useless.

During their history of ocean living sea snakes have developed vertically flattened tails that give them considerable thrust against the water as they undulate their bodies in their swimming motion. Most of the time they move slowly, but, like eels, they can double their speed if necessary.

Snakes that live in desert areas naturally have a problem trying to make progress on loose sand. Body thrusts of the conventional snake movement would merely push the sand aside, or down, and they would remain more or less stationary, so they have had to adopt a quite different kind of motion. This has given them the name *sidewinder*.

They throw the body into lateral curves, and when moving only two points of the body touch the ground. These two points remain stationary while the raised parts move at an angle to the direction of the undulations passing along the body. The point of contact starts at the head end and proceeds backward as in any other snake, but instead of moving straight forward, the animal moves diagonally. An illustration of this can be seen in Figure 25.

25. *The sidewinder* (Crotalus cerastes), *unable to grip loose sand with its ventral scales, must undulate in a diagonal direction to make forward progress.*

Chapter 9
THE EARLIEST MAMMALS

When trying to identify the ancestral mammals, one is uncertain whether to call them mammallike reptiles or reptilelike mammals. One may have to accept the former definition, because they appeared even before the giant reptiles some 225 million years ago or more, but they were slow to reach their dominant position. They still looked like and walked like reptiles, even though some essential limb changes were taking place. There were also some very large species, although the mammalian stock probably sprang mostly from very small ones.

One of the most important changes that began to take place in these animals was in the position and attitudes of the limbs. They sprawled less and were brought more under the body, and the muscles and backbone assumed a more mammalian form. The toes became more equal in length, and with diet modifications and changing habits the mammalian appearance slowly developed—in many of them somewhat like present-day monotremes.

The Changes Begin

One of these ancestors, *thrinaxodon,* a lightly built active carnivore, almost a mammal, demonstrates a number of changes that took place as the mammals evolved in the Triassic period 200 million years ago. It seems to have been neatly transitional in its skeletal features between reptiles and mammals.

True mammals probably began to appear about 160 million years ago, but they made little progress in numbers until the giant reptiles disappeared. Their survival must have been due to a greater adaptability than other contemporary animals had, and this adaptability may have been the result of their becoming warm-blooded, which made them less dependent on climate or temperature.

One of the changes in the limbs of these early mammals was the position of the cartilage from which bone tissue grows. This put a limit to the amount of growth possible, instead of allowing growth to be continuous, as in reptiles. At the same time countless other changes took place in teeth, organs, tail, ribs, and so on.

The limbs continued to develop toward the modern mammalian positions under the body, adopting a straight forward gait, the muscles and their attachments changing to produce this. The feet and hands of some early species seem to have had a certain amount of grasping power and were probably armed with claws. All this aided in the development of greater speed, especially as a flat-on-the-ground foot position gave way to one in which animals poised more on their toes, like the modern cat, dog, and horse. Some mammalian forms took to flying and gliding, and some returned to the sea.

What we know as true placental mammals did not appear in any considerable numbers until about 70 million years ago, when the mammallike reptiles had already been very rare for 70 or 80 million years, and other primitive mammals, most of them very small, had existed for almost 100 million years. What is important for us to realize is that it took maybe 150 million years for the present limb formations to be perfected from the awkward lumbering reptilian forms prominent when mammals first evolved.

Chapter 10
WALKING AND RUNNING ON LAND

Mammalian Limbs

Most mammals that actively pursue prey on land, and those that are hunted, too, have limbs adapted for fast running and sudden leaping movements. The toes are armed with claws that, in the cat family, can be extended or withdrawn; they are retractable. There are five digits in the hand or front foot, and usually four in the hind foot. No carnivore has less than four digits.

The weight of heavy animals like the rhinoceros and elephant is usually supported by massive pillarlike limbs and large feet composed of a varying number of digits. The arch of the foot is supported by a pad of elastic tissue. It was mentioned in Chapter 9 that in the primitive foot the entire sole rested on the ground. This is known as a *plantigrade* foot. Relatively few existing terrestrial mammals have retained this posture, but it is very obvious in bears.

The primitive framework from which all mammalian limbs are derived consists of three major segments: an upper arm, forearm, and hand in the forelimb, and a thigh, leg, and foot in the hind limb. The forelimb or arm is joined to the trunk by a ball-and-socket articulation between the head of the *humerus* (upper-arm bone) and a cuplike cavity in the *scapula* (shoulder blade). The hind limb is similarly at-

26. *The hippopotamus* (A) *and the llama* (B) *are two examples of even-toed* (artiodactylus) *ungulate animals. They are in contrast to the horse, which is odd-toed in having only one toe, the hoof, and the rhinoceros* (C), *which has three toes, and are therefore* perissodactylus.

tached at the hip by a joint between the head of the *femur* (upper leg bone) and the *acetabulum* (socket) in the *pelvis*. Elbow and knee joints are hingelike in their movement, and only allow comparatively restricted flexibility.

The hand is jointed to the forearm by *carpal* (wrist) bones (refer to Figure 1), and the foot is jointed to the leg by *tarsal* (ankle) bones, all consisting of irregularly shaped bones that allow considerable flexibility. Between their joints and the digits (fingers and toes) there are five *metacarpals* in the hand, and five *metatarsals* in the foot, so the third segment of each limb consists of three series of bones: the *phalanges* in the fingers and toes, the metacarpals in the wrist and metatarsals in the ankle, and the carpus or tarsus.

Using one of the big cats as an example, contraction of the *triceps* muscle in its foreleg pulls up the insertion on the funny bone (*olecranon process of the ulnar*). At the same time the *biceps* muscle relaxes, allowing the elbow joint to open, and this straightens the limb. (See Figure 2.)

Thrust from the hind limbs in land mammals is transmitted at the hip joints to the pelvis, which is firmly fixed to a group of vertebrae known as the *sacrum*. This and the form of the hind limbs may vary considerably between groups, but the same principal elements can always be distinguished.

When the average quadruped stands still, the center of pressure of each limb lies vertically under the center of rotation of the joint by which that limb articulates. However, the center of gravity naturally lies elsewhere, and the location of this is important for walking and running. In the horse, for instance, we can see that for the front leg to be lifted, the weight must be thrown back slightly, and vice versa for the rear legs, for which the center of gravity must lie slightly forward.

Again, speaking of typical quadrupeds, half the weight of the body is carried on the two left legs, and half on the right, but it is not necessarily equal for all four limbs, since the center of gravity may be closer to the front limbs, and in that case there will be greater muscular development in front.

This changes when running. As hinted earlier, the centers of gravity and pressure change position as the limbs change their angles to the body. Otherwise jointed limbs are always in a vertical line with centers of pressure.

When walking slowly, a horse (and some other animals) always has three feet on the ground, so that each limb moves individually. In normal walking, the horse balances alternately on two feet on the same side of the body and on a pair diagonally opposed to each other. When it trots it uses diagonally opposite feet, and when it gallops it never has more than any two feet on the ground simultaneously.

Adaptations for running characteristic of the horse, zebra, and similar animals are comparable with those of deer and other even-toed hoofed animals. But horses have only a single digit (the hoof) on each foot, whereas some of the others may have either two or four digits, each usually sheathed in a cornified hoof. Examples of these are seen in the hippopotamus, camels, pigs, et cetera.

In a plantigrade hind limb like that of a bear, the center of rotation of the hip joint lies vertically over the center of pressure of the foot on the ground—over the ankle and heel. That is when the foot is flat

27. *The left rear leg of this bear shows the hip joint lying vertically above the center of pressure of the foot when the weight of the body is thrown on this foot, so that the other legs can swing into a fresh position.*

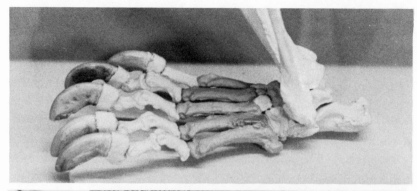

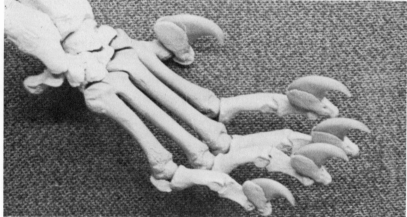

28. *The skeletons of a bear's and a tiger's forefeet show clearly the difference between a plantigrade foot* (top) *and a digitigrade foot, which carries the weight on the toes only.*

on the ground only. But the center of rotation is moved to above the toes when the heel is raised in walking slowly. Similarly the shoulder lies vertically over the wrist or ankle in the forelimb, and moves to above the toes in slow walking.

When a bear rears up on its hind limbs it brings its entire center of gravity over its hind feet, whereas when on all fours it is probably slightly ahead of center. In other animals the movement of the limb parts varies with the species and with its speed. In some the greater part of the weight falls on their forelimbs; in others, on their hind limbs.

Dogs and other mammals like them walk only on their digits; not on soles and palms, and the number of toes is often reduced. This is therefore called a *digitigrade* foot. Such a posture gives speed and agility, but is quite unsuitable for weight-carrying. Hoofed animals walking on modified nails or hooves are called *unguligrade,* and these show all the gradations of foot posture from a semiplantigrade condition in some to the high stiltlike development found in a few antelopes. When the digits used are reduced to a single pair, the whole limb is specialized for high-speed running.

Speed of Movement

The rate of acceleration an animal can produce depends on its weight and the backward thrust of its powerful leg muscles. Usually, the higher the speed, the shorter the time this can be maintained, even in a horse or a wolf, or any similar running animal; and the more calories the animal uses up in an hour. Often a smaller animal can move at much the same speed as a larger one because the latter must have more powerful limbs and muscles to produce equal performance. A good example of this is seen in the horse and the greyhound.

Other factors in the speed of an animal depend on the length of its legs, the frequency of their stride, the speed the body travels between the time a limb leaves the ground and hits it again, and the extent to which the animal can bow its body during each stride.

One scientist, Gray, has devised a formula for calculating man's energy expenditure when running, and this can be applied to many other animals. It is

$$AR = \frac{E}{T} + ET,$$

when AR is the maximum average rate of energy expenditure, E is the available energy, T is the time of the effect, and ET is the energy that can be made available in the time.

Power and Temperature

It is considered that every ten-degree Celsius rise in body temperature doubles the output of power from muscles, so this raises an interesting point of comparison between warm-blooded marine mammals and cold-blooded fish, and between warm-blooded land mammals and cold-blooded reptiles. In the case of marine mammals, speed is related to other factors, all of which are discussed in Chapter 5, and reptiles, because they depend on warm air to provide their body heat, can function only above certain temperatures. Many land mammals, on the other hand, can function within a very wide range of temperatures, sometimes varying 100 degrees on the Fahrenheit scale (about 55 degrees Celsius) because they manufacture their own body heat and also have mechanisms for body cooling, all depending on the efficiency of the circulatory system, which keeps the body temperature constant.

When all these things are considered, it is obvious that reptiles are probably the only animals to which such a relationship between body temperature and performance can apply. Fish are so critical in their response to temperature rise and fall that most can only accept a few degrees without dying; and mammals that had an increase in body temperature of ten degrees Celsius would probably be in the throes of a fatal fever.

But reptiles respond very obviously to warmth and cold. As temperature drops they become torpid, and as it rises they become much more active and fast moving, until the temperature reaches a point when they seek shelter from it. Mammals, however, seek shelter from heat very soon after it passes the level of their normal body temperature; and some of them even before that.

The increased speed of movement that reptiles enjoy with a rising temperature must of course come from increased power, and this is the result of the increasing level of metabolism that higher temperatures always bring.

Hopping Mammals

Mammals that travel by jumping have small arms, very long hind legs, and well-developed tails that act as a counterpoise. In many animals the tails also act as a third leg, or at least a prop when the animal is at rest. In the family of kangaroos, the foot has gained the extra leverage required for leaping by elongation of the metatarsal of the fourth toe. The kangaroo uses only the fourth and fifth toes; the second and third being small and joined within the skin. A crest on the front of the tibia provides attachment for the powerful muscles involved in leaping.

There are some very considerable advantages to the kangaroo's method of locomotion. At higher speeds, the metabolic act is much lower than for quadrupedal running, although it may be higher at low speeds. This is partly because higher speeds do not necessarily involve more hops in a given time; only longer hops. The same applies to mice. Hopping mice are much more economical of energy than quadrupedal mice.

Another advantage to hopping is the ability to produce a sudden burst of speed from a standing start, and movement in an unpredictable direction. We see this in so many other kinds of animal too—frogs, grasshoppers, fleas, and so on.

29. *A kangaroo's foot uses the fourth and fifth toes* (center *and* left) *to give it traction. The second* (very small) *and third toes are joined together within the skin.*

Specialized Mammalian Limbs

Mammals that live in trees often do very little actual walking, although they may come down to the ground and show considerable agility there. Most of the time they use their efficient grasping hands and feet to move or swing from branch to branch. We call them *brachiators* because of this grasping habit.

Their arms are frequently much longer than their legs, and when walking, their plantigrade gait is awkward, the weight of the body being borne on the outer sides of the feet and the knuckles of the hands. All the apes walk like this, but not all the tree-living primates.

In *tarsiers,* which jump from branch to branch rather than swing, the heel and ankle bones are greatly elongated, increasing the leverage of the jumping muscles. Suckerlike disks at the ends of the fingers and toes provide a sure grip on landing. The nails on their hands and feet are retained only for grooming.

When compared with those of the apes, man's hands and feet pre-

30. *The rear legs of a jerboa like this* Allactaga euphratica *can produce sudden bursts of energetic movement and unpredictable direction. They also permit a greater economy of energy than is possible to a quadrupedal animal and can take leaps up to six feet in length.*

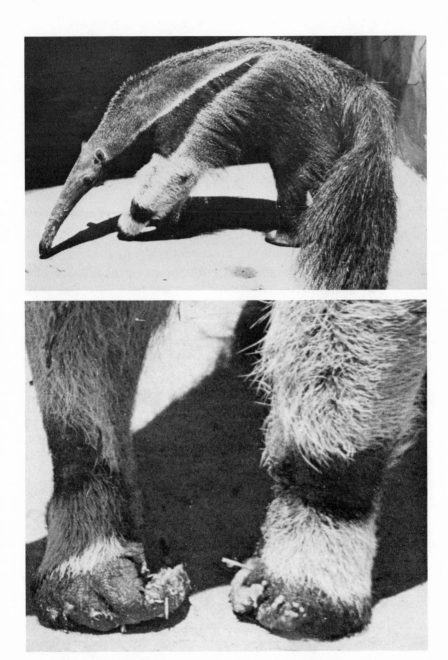

31. *The giant anteater* (Myrmecophaga jubata) *bears the weight of the front of its body on the backs of its digits.*

sent some considerable differences. Man's legs and feet are as nearly as possible immediately below the center of gravity for his body, the knees close together. The axis of the tibia makes a right angle with the ankle joint, whereas in apes the angle is acuter. Man's foot bones form an arch, and the weight is transferred from the leg onto both heel and toes. No trace of an arch appears in ape feet. A distinctly human feature is the large size of the first toe and its inability to act in opposition to the other toes like the ape toes can.

Though in no way like an ape, another animal that bears its weight on the backs of its fingers and the soles of its hind feet is the giant anteater (*Myrmecophaga jubata*). Prominent ridges on the long bones of the forelimbs provide attachment for the powerful muscles this animal uses to dig into solid anthills. The middle digit has a large claw, the main tool for this digging.

The limbs of all burrowing mammals are short and very powerful. Badgers (*Meles spp.* and *Taxidea spp.*), wombats (*Phascolarctos spp.*), marmots (*Marmota spp.*), and moles (*Talpa spp.*) are examples which come quickly to mind. Perhaps a few animals burrow with more proportionate legs, but often these only trim already existing burrows dug by other truly burrowing animals.

Running Flightless Birds

Some of those birds that for various reasons have abandoned the use of their wings have instead developed powerful legs with which they can often run at very considerable speeds. The Australian emu (*Dromaius novaehollandiae*) can run at more than 30 mph, the ring-necked pheasant (*Phasianus colchicus*) at more than 20 mph, and the roadrunner (*Geococcyx californianus*) at only slightly less.

New Zealand is the home of many flightless birds, largely because of the small animal population, absence of predation, and 70 million years of complete isolation from contact with other lands. Prior to that time there was evidently a land bridge between New Zealand and other islands across which the present birds' ancestors traveled.

32. *The short, powerful limbs of the echidna* (Tachyglossus aculeatus) *are clearly visible here, especially in the skeleton below.*

One of the earliest arrivals was the kiwi (*Apteryx spp.*) which even at that time was evidently flightless, and may have descended from the same ancestors as the moa, ostrich, emu, and rhea. The modern kiwi has powerful legs and will range in all kinds of territory, but its long history of freedom from predation has not encouraged it to develop any considerable running speed, although it is not slow.

33. *The degenerate wings and heavy body of the kiwi* (Apteryx spp.) *have de-manded the development of powerful legs.*

Another bird with a similar build and leisurely movements is the weka (*Gallirallus australis*). Both it and the kiwi have allowed their wings to degenerate until they are really only vestigial. There are others on the same downward path to flightlessness, but which as yet are not entirely incapable of using their wings to a slight extent. The kakapo (*Strigops habroptilus*), a ground parrot, can make short downward glides of up to one hundred yards, but it is unable to make a flapping flight. Its feet and legs are strong, however, and it can climb with considerable agility.

The pukeka (*Porphyrio melanotus*) can still fly short distances, but it is a heavy bird, and relies more on its ability to run rapidly on powerful legs.

There are very few flightless running birds in other countries. The ostrich (*Struthio camelus*), found in Africa and Arabia, is a powerful

34. The three-toed foot of a cassowary (Casuarius casuarius), left, *and the two-toed foot of an ostrich* (Struthio camelus).

bird that can run up to 35 mph on feet that have retained only two toes. The rhea (*Rhea americana*) of the South American pampas and savannas, which has three toes webbed at the base, is another fast runner.

The roadrunner mentioned earlier can actually fly, but only very awkwardly; instead it uses its wings and tail for balancing and maneuvering as it runs, often taking up to twelve steps a second to achieve its extreme agility.

These running birds are called *ratites,* and they have lost many of the features of flying birds as they have gained weight. In flying birds, the sternum or breastbone is keeled to take the powerful flying muscles necessary for sustained flight; the ratites do not have this, their sternums are flat. The flying birds also have hollow bones and air cavities throughout the body; the ratites do not have these either. The large ratites, such as the ostrich, being unable to escape predators by flying, have developed tremendous kicking power in their legs, and the immense main toe claw has become a very formidable weapon.

Part IV

FLYING AND GLIDING

Chapter 11

THE EVOLUTION
OF VARIOUS WING FORMS

Flight has some undeniable advantages that earthbound creatures can never enjoy. First, it permits sudden and rapid escape from enemies, and of course just as sudden and rapid pouncing on prey. Second, it permits penetration into places inaccessible to nonfliers. Third, it allows fast straight-line travel from one spot to another. Fourth, it facilitates migration over long distances by day or night; and finally it permits an uninterrupted view of all beneath and over great distances. Not for nothing do birds have the most acute vision in the entire animal world.

But these advantages all make special demands on birds, such as the need for exceedingly rapid reactions, fast and powerful muscle action, and accurate judgment. It is also necessary for birds to have very light weight, and this demands an easily injured skeleton, the slightest break in which will result in the bird's being unable to feed itself or escape from predators.

Skin Wings

The first flying creatures, which were reptilian ancestors of our modern birds, must have been very clumsy, and almost certainly they

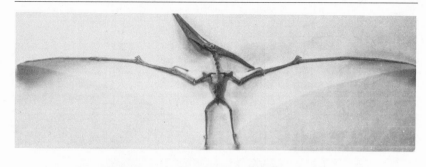

35. Top, *a* Pteranodon longiceps, *and* below, *a pterodactyl, two of the earliest gliding reptiles, all of which disappeared about 65 million years ago.*

could only glide from tree to tree or from tree to ground, from where they climbed up again. We can tell this in fossils, by the way the humerus was articulated, and also by the length and form of the fingers, since these were involved in the wing structure.

Pteranodon longiceps, which we might call a reptilian bird, had only membranous wings rather like those of a bat. They were operated by an up-and-down movement of the humerus, so they were almost certainly used only for gliding. This creature's 18–25-foot wingspan would have been ideal for gliding, but not for flapping. Any tear in a wing membrane would have grounded a pteranodon anyway, and once grounded it would have been too clumsy to survive.

Not all of the reptilian birds of the period were so large. There were species of pterodactyl as small as sparrows, but large or small, they all died out about 65 million years ago.

The archaeopteryx, which lived in Europe more than 120 million years ago, was probably mostly a glider, too, even though it had feathers on its body, wings, and tail. Its skeleton was still very reptilian, and it lacked the keeled breastbone and muscles needed for flapping flight. Only two specimens of this bird ancestor have so far been found, both in the same district in Bavaria (Germany).

Both the archaeopteryx and the pteranodon evolved from reptiles that had learned to run fast on their hind legs only, but because the archaeopteryx was more birdlike in having feathers, it probably had warmer blood as well. How the feathers evolved is still a mystery. It seems that they were modifications of lizard scales, but no transition stage from one to the other has yet been identified.

36. *The archaeopteryx, possibly the first feathered glider, which, however, was still very reptilian in other ways.*

Feathers and other Essentials

Feathers are one of the features that enabled birds to become efficient flying machines, but other features were just as necessary: hollow (lightweight) bones, a large heart, powerful wing muscles, and an unusual breathing system, all of which produce a high power to low weight ratio. This ratio is augmented even further by very high-caloric foods.

So many of the first flying and gliding birds had formidable teeth that they must have been carnivorous, but others moving into territory where a carnivorous diet was less possible had to turn to other high-protein and high-calorie foods, such as seeds, fruits, nuts, worms, and insects, and these habits have persisted. But different prey means different environments, and these demand different wing forms.

Functional Wings

Birds such as crows, doves, woodpeckers, and passerines, which are adapted to forested areas where maneuvering must be accurate and tight, will naturally need a differently functioning wing type from birds that feed on the wing in the open at high speed, like swifts and swallows, hummingbirds, and falcons, or those that make long migrations.

The wings of the migrators are flatter and usually taper to a finer tip, sweeping back very much like those of a modern swing-wing airplane. Different again must be the wings of soaring ocean birds like the albatross and petrels, which must have wings with a high ratio of length to width, like mechanical gliders. But this does not apply to land soarers like vultures, hawks, and eagles, which must also carry heavy loads back to their nests for young. These require a more moderate length-to-width ratio and a deep camber. Their wings must also be well slotted. (See Figure 37, and Chapter 12.)

The difference between these two kinds of soaring wings is mainly that the ocean soarers are involved with high speed, low altitude, and dynamic soaring on air currents, whereas the land soarers are more involved with low speeds and high altitudes. Gliding from high altitudes is easier with a heavy body and relatively small wings than with the larger wings of the ocean soarers.

As well as different wing shapes for different purposes, the length and flexibility of feathers and the size and power of wing muscles have evolved to suit each of these purposes. We can say that wings have therefore evolved into at least seven forms, giving the following skills:

1. Flapping flight
2. Soaring
3. Hovering
4. Swooping
5. Diving
6. Launching
7. Underwater swimming

The last form is dealt with separately in Chapter 6.

Reverting to the evolutionary aspects of birds' wings, it is difficult to visualize how the first flying reptiles with wings consisting merely of skin membranes could have launched themselves into the air from the ground. They must have done so from trees or ledges, like the present flying mammals do, climbing back up with vestigial claws on their wings.

Not until feathered birds like the archaeopteryx began to show new and improved forms could ground-launching become possible. Then, the wings became structures on short upper arms and long forearms with three very reduced digits at their ends (the other two were discarded), and all bearing large quills to give the wings their lightweight lifting surfaces. The sternum (breastbone) became enlarged, and the scapula modified.

By Cretaceous times, which spanned the period from 120 million to 60 million years ago, we find seabirds well established. There were also land birds and divers very much like modern types, some even having allowed their wings to degenerate for a return to aquatic life, so it is obvious that the evolution of most wing forms took place more than 60 million years ago, and possibly 100 million years ago.

From then on, evolutionary trends were in two directions: toward better flight control in most, and to flightlessness with increased size and weight in another group. Birds have been one of the world's largest vertebrate groups since the Cretaceous period. A clearer picture of the various wing forms that have evolved will appear in Chapter 12, where their various functions are discussed more fully.

Chapter 12
THE MECHANICS
OF FLIGHT

Flight does not just involve the flapping of wings, or even the necessary possession of feathers. It was mentioned in Chapter 11 that specialized bones, muscles, air sacs, and vital organs also play an important part in flight, and these can now be dealt with in greater detail.

Reduced Body Weight

Although the use of wings appears to be the dominant feature of flight, the skeleton must also be unusually light and strong. This is achieved by having hollow bones of extreme thinness filled with air like the quills of feathers. In other words, the skeleton consists of openwork structures having the same outward appearance as the solid bones of nonflying animals.

For instance, the skeleton of a pigeon is said to account for only 4.4 percent of its body weight in spite of the fact that any flying bird must have stronger pectoral and pelvic girdles than other animals. Despite its lightness the skeleton is strong and somewhat flexible. The bones are also welded together.

The very thin bones of the skull, which is often no more than a fiftieth of a bird's body weight, are trussed with fine strutting, and this is also found in the larger bones of the wings. The sternum is a thin flat keel for the attachment of the large wing muscles, and the size of this sternum in a fossil bird skeleton tells us to what extent it was able to fly.

A bird's weight is further reduced by the absence of a urinary bladder. Its kidneys excrete nitrogenous wastes instead of urine, and these pass into the cloaca for release with other alimentary waste. Bird metabolism is also high, much higher than in land animals, and this increases the body temperature, which in some is as high as 110.5°F. (43.5°C.). Fuel burning is so rapid that food may pass through a bird's entire digestive system in a matter of minutes, and this provides high power almost instantly.

A bird's respiratory system is also part of its weight-reducing mechanism. In addition to lungs, birds possess an accessory system usually consisting of five pairs of air sacs connected with the lungs. These branch through the body and even enter the larger bones to occupy their hollow interiors.

The air sacs supplement the lungs by increasing the availability and use of oxygen, and they also serve as a cooling system for the fast metabolism that operates during flight. Combined with the lungs, these air sacs often make up 20 percent of the entire body volume, four times as much as in humans.

Flying Muscles

The breast muscles that drive the bird's wings are often a very large percentage of its body weight—in the pigeon, for instance, up to 50 percent. But in the high fliers, like the condors and vultures, which glide or soar, the breast muscles are not so massive. These birds rely more on tendons and ligaments to hold their wings in the soaring position.

To accomplish its two basic functions, propulsion and lift, a typical wing must drive the body through the air and at the same time neutralize gravity. Its construction is thickest and rounded at the leading edge, where it has bones that give it rigidity and strength, and it tapers to a thin trailing edge at the rear. Covert feathers give it a rounded, smooth, streamlined contour.

Two groups of muscles work the wings. A *pectoralis minor* muscle originates from the flat part of the breastbone close to the side of the keel, passing forward and then upward through a pulley hole on the inner side of the shoulder joint to join the upper arm bone (humerus). Contracting this muscle over the pulley raises the wing.

The downstroke of the wing is accomplished by the contraction of a massive *pectoralis major* muscle, which has its origin both on the keel and the breast at the side of the attachment of the pectoralis minor. It passes straight outward and is fixed to the front edge of the humerus.

Wing Contours

In sectional form, a bird's wing is arched or convex above and hollow or concave below, a form that automatically creates a strong upward suction as it passes through the air. This creates the lift that neutralizes the downward pull of gravity and the weak suction that develops below the wing. In active flight, the main part of the wing creating this lift is the inner part, or upper-arm section. Forward propulsion is by the hand part, or outer section of the wing.

The cambering contour of a wing is especially pronounced in slow fliers, and because the rear edge of a wing is much more flexible with its long feathers than the leading edge, it tends to bend upward from the pressure below it and adds to the forward drive of the end of the wing with each downward stroke.

Wing Feathers and Tail

The contour, shape, and size of a wing depend very greatly on the number and size of feathers it supports, or which, perhaps more accurately, support it. Feathers overlap each other rather like shingles on a roof so that the fairly rigid leading edge of any one feather lies

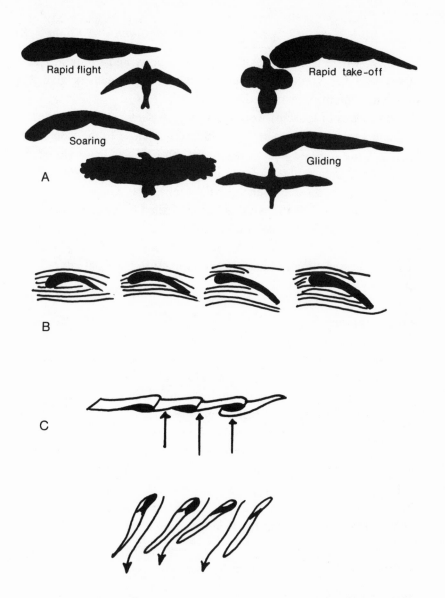

37. Section A *shows the wing contours and silhouettes of birds using the flight patterns described in the text.* Section B *shows how the changing attitude of a wing affects the air flow over its surface and creates greater lift. In* section C (top) *the downstroke of a wing forces up the rear edges of feathers into an unbroken surface, but when they open* (bottom) *on the upstroke, they allow air to pass through with a minimum of resistance.*

above the less rigid trailing edge of the next one (in front of it). This arrangement locks into a solid surface that does not let any air through on the downstroke, but which opens like a venetian blind to let air flow through on the upstroke.

The feathers on the hand or tip end of a wing are known as *primaries*. Those closer to the bird's body are known as *secondaries*, and are attached to the forearm (ulna). The primaries are the more essential to flight, and they are much larger than secondaries. The removal of even the smallest piece of a primary wing feather will upset a bird's ability to fly, and damage to several of them may even

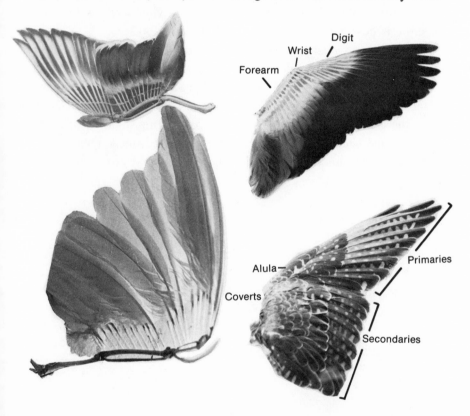

38. *The disposition of the feathers on a wing, together with the length and strength of supporting bones, is related to the kind of flight the bird needs.*

prevent flying altogether, whereas it is possible for a bird's flight to be almost unaffected by the removal of as much as half the secondary feathers.

Most birds have ten primaries on each wing. This number varies between nine and twelve if one considers all genera, but there is much greater variation in the secondaries, which range from six to thirty-two in number, the higher numbers being on the long wings of ocean soarers.

There is a tuft of feathers on the thumb bone of the wing known as the *alula*. During normal flight it lies flat against the body of the wing, but during takeoff and landing, when flying speed is low and stalling is possible, this is used to add to lifting potential.

Not only are feathers tightly closed during the downstroke of a wing, and opened into slots to reduce air resistance in the forward upstroke, but they also bend upward with each downstroke. This produces the same kind of effect as the pitch in a propeller blade. Then, too, the tail feathers play an important part during flight in ensuring stability and balance. They can be raised, lowered, made concave, or angled in any direction to provide the necessary steering motion in maneuvering.

Flight

Lifting power equal to half the weight of a bird must be provided by each of its wings, and these must also produce a propulsive force that is greater than the drag or air resistance to the bird's body. Three factors are important in this:

1. The angle of a wing in relation to the airstream
2. The shape of a wing
3. The area of a wing

The essential contours of a wing, convex above and concave below, have already been described, and now we can examine the dynamic reasons why these are so important.

If the two sides of a wing, upper and lower, were equal, the resistance to air or air pressure would also be equal. Flattening or making the lower side concave and lengthening the upper side by making it convex reduces the pressure on the upper side and increases it on the lower. The lift thus created is increased still further if the forward edge of a wing is raised higher than the rear edge, and it is again increased when the rear edge is thinner than the leading edge, because this decreases air drag.

The very wide wingspan of narrow-winged birds like the albatross (*Diomedia exulans*), in which the length of the wing is up to eighteen times its width, produces very little drag, and a tremendous lift that may be as much as forty times the drag. This permits what is known as *dynamic soaring,* which is the most economical of energy of any kind of flight because it uses different adjacent lifting air currents.

Flapping Flight

When a small bird takes off from the ground or its perch, its wing strokes operate in the manner described earlier, but this is not always so in large birds, and a little repetition is necessary to demonstrate the differences. The small bird's wings move down and forward in the downstroke, and the trailing edge, being more flexible than the leading edge, bends upward to operate like a propeller and pulls the bird forward through the air. The return stroke, upward and backward, produces negligible propulsion because the primary feathers separate to produce slots through which the air slips. (See Figure 37.)

In larger birds, no matter how well streamlined their bodies may be, one of the most important factors is the ratio of body weight to wingspan. Larger wings mean fewer strokes per second because the larger muscles cannot operate so rapidly against the greater areas of air resistance, so both the up and down wingstrokes must work to lift or propel the bird.

The downstroke has a pulling action, as it does in smaller birds, but the upstroke bends the wing at the wrist and elbow so that the whole arm rotates backward at the shoulder joint. This makes the primary feathers push against the air with their upper surfaces and add more forward drive to that created by the downstroke. At the end of the upstroke, the wing is rotated forward in such a way that the primary feathers snap back, ready for the next downstroke.

The path described by the wing tips when seen from the side describes an oval or a figure eight in a full down-and-up excursion, the major axis of the configuration being downward and forward in the direction of flight. It was said earlier that the tail controls turning, banking, and change of flight direction, but in many birds the wings assist this quite actively, and in some even the feet are used as an aid. The tail, however, is most important in rapid maneuvers, those birds with short tails having the most unwavering flight paths.

When a bird uses its tail to bank or roll, this changes the effect of the wings on the air. If, for instance, the bird turns to the left, the right wing travels farther and faster than the left, and it so produces more lift, aiding in the tilting of the body in the banking motion. Understanding this makes it clear why birds with small wings and short tails cannot make sharp turns. Ducks are an example of this kind of bird.

Briefly summarizing this section on flight, we can say that strongly arched wings provide the greatest lift and are most prevalent in woodland birds, which must take off in a short space and climb steeply to avoid undergrowth. These birds usually have short broad wings. High-soaring birds have highly arched wings also, but in their case they are of great width and span. A large wing area with a relatively light body is essential for soaring flight. Ocean soarers, on the other hand, have a large wingspan but do not have so much breadth in their wings because they must have more agility, and they only soar at low levels.

Hovering

The hummingbird's body slants up at about a 45-degree angle when it is flying, so the plane of its wingbeats is virtually horizontal. As its wings move up and back, and then down and forward, their upper and lower surfaces face downward alternately. This is made possible by an unusual degree of rotation in the humerus and its insertion. Although all birds except swifts articulate their wings at the shoulder, elbow, and wrist, the hummingbird uses its shoulder almost exclusively, the wings rotating more like those of an insect.

The hummingbird's wing therefore operates very much like a helicopter rotor blade, forcing air downward with both up and downstrokes and enabling the bird to rise straight up, hover, or even back off. This tiny bird requires such great wing power and speed of wingbeat that its breast muscles make up 30 percent of its entire body weight.

When flying in flocks, birds use each other's energy like fish swimming in shoals. They take advantage of the lift turbulence created by the motion of those in front of them, just as fish coast in each other's current eddies.

Dynamic Soaring

The albatross glides down on the wind from high to low levels, giving itself momentum to turn head-on into the wind again and use this to climb back to a higher level on its upcurrent. In this way it can cover vast distances without once flapping its wings. The long, narrow wings of these marine soaring birds also permit very high speeds when they are gliding. Ospreys, for instance, have been timed gliding at 80 mph.

Not only albatross, but gulls and petrels too glide low over the water into the wind as it is deflected up by waves that are a little warmer than the air above. They glide from the still air in the wave troughs into the wind blowing over the crests. Without appreciable waves and troughs, these birds fly into the wind and soar, losing speed but gaining height before turning and gliding downwind to increase speed again, turning into the wind once more when close to the water surface.

Thermal Soaring

Seabirds that use dynamic soaring seldom fly high. Only land birds can soar to great heights, because the temperature over land varies much more than over water, so powerful thermal upcurrents can be used instead of the gentle air upcurrents present over waves. Land birds such as hawks, eagles, vultures, and condors that use these thermal currents have broad wings and fanlike tails, in contrast to the extremely long, narrow wings and small tails of the ocean birds.

Thermal-soaring birds ride the warm air currents by spiraling in circles or loops on full extended motionless wings, continuously gaining height. The ideal upcurrents occur on mountainsides and over hot deserts. When gliding down, the birds flex their wings back to reduce both their area and their span, thus increasing the pull of gravity and giving them speed.

Diving

Fishing birds, which dive, and falcons, which strike (stoop) at the end of a high-speed dive, spread and curve their tails to increase the lift at the rear end of the body and tip the head downward. The speed of dive is controlled by the degree of flexing of the wings, which may even be folded right back to the body until the moment for braking arrives.

Launching into Flight

Birds take off in several different ways. From open ground or over the surface of water, most rise into the wind, large birds gaining momentum by making a short run before pushing off strongly when their wing rhythm has reached a critical speed. Many birds, especially small birds or those with weaker legs, launch themselves by dropping from a height to give themselves momentum, using a ledge or a tree branch or a building.

39. *An eagle diving onto an arctic hare. Tail is spread wide for braking and tilting the body; wings are arched and wide open for braking and lift, and feet are held forward, ready to grasp its prey.*

Long-legged waders have their bodies high enough off the ground to be able to launch themselves with powerful wings and a single push with their legs. Some big birds, especially vultures, will regurgitate food or empty their bowels in order to lighten their weight and take off in an emergency.

Once a bird levels off in full flight, its wings do not beat as strongly as when gaining height and speed. The wing strokes become almost vertical, the inner segments of the wings almost stationary and horizontal, while the outer ends, the hands, do most of the flapping, bending at the wrists, and acting like propellers.

Landing

When a bird approaches its landing site, it lowers its speed by bending its body until its tail and wings are vertical, the tail feathers spread fanlike, and the wings outstretched with the alula opened to reduce stalling. It then drops gently with its feet held forward, ready for landing. If extra braking is necessary, it beats its wings against its direction of movement.

Some birds that cannot reduce their speed enough for a gentle landing avoid injury by dropping below their target and allowing themselves to be lifted up to it by the resistance of the air to their momentum. When landing on the ground, a bird will angle its body up at right angles to the direction of its flight, spreading its wings and tail, and then beating its wings rapidly against the air in the last yard or so.

Chapter 13
FISH DECIDE TO FLY

Although in the Triassic period (up to 190 million years ago), there were still some ancient armored fish warding off extinction, some fish had already taken to leaping from the water as the forerunners of our present so-called flying fish. One, *Thoracopterus niederristi,* was an unmistakable glider. Modern species glide in the same way by spreading their winglike pectoral and pelvic fins, which fold back against the body when the fish are swimming.

The Takeoff

Some species are such expert gliders after leaving the water that they can travel a considerable distance before dropping into the water again. They rush through the water toward the surface and launch themselves into the air at speeds of 20 mph or more, spreading their winglike fins as they leave the water. They never flap these fins; the muscles that serve them will only raise and lower them.

Most flying fish live in tropical and subtropical seas. They are branches of the herring family, and this means they are tasty prey for larger fish and seabirds, and because of this attraction for predators they have evolved their air-gliding as an escape device. In addition

40. *Flying fish really glide by spreading their enlarged pectoral and pelvic fins after takeoff with a rushing leap from the water. This is a specimen of Cypsilurinae.*

to their enlarged fins, which in some species spread up to twenty inches, most of these fish have an extended lower lobe to the tail. This lobe remains in the water and beats frantically from side to side until the fish is supported by the wind under its large fins. Then the tail leaves the water surface.

It is possible for this tail-beating launch pattern to be repeated several times before a fish reenters the water, and this can keep it airborne for up to 20 seconds. Some remarkable recordings have been made of such flights. One measured a launching speed of 35 mph, and the gliding time of some of them has been clocked at more than 40 seconds. An incredible gliding height of 50 feet has also been quoted.

My own personal observations of thousands of these fish have never recorded them as going higher than five or six feet, but they have certainly been found stranded on the deck of the ship at a height of about 20 feet early in the morning, and they sometimes have entered through portholes.

There are two kinds of these fish, Exocoetidae, in which the pectoral fins alone provide all the lift, and Cypselurinae, in which the pelvic fins assist them. This last group shoot toward the surface of the water with the fins folded at the sides of the body, and then, as the front end of the body leaves the water, the pectoral fins open and the tail beats frantically to gain speed; then as the rest of the body leaves the water, the pelvic fins open out.

The flights of this group are very fast. Although they do not usually last more than about 12 seconds, they are said to be able to cover 220 to 440 yards. A fish will often land on its tail, beat its tail fiercely, and then take off again, heading into the wind. One fish, *Gasteropelecus*, moves its pectoral fins as a seeming flight aid, but although its pectoral muscles amount to 25 percent of its body weight, it is still not capable of true flight; it can only glide.

Leapers and Flappers

Many other kinds of fish without abnormally developed fins can leap out of and skitter along the water surface. Garfish (*Lepistosteus spp.*) do it, and so do halfbeaks (*Hyporhamphus unifasciatus*), which can glide for 40 feet. Like true gliding fish, they vibrate their tails violently to keep themselves above water and moving. In the Indo-Pacific region, a species with somewhat enlarged pectoral fins is said to glide up to 50 yards.

What might almost be called a true flying fish is found in fresh water. Two species, the hatchet fish (*Gasteropelecus*), which was mentioned earlier, and the butterfly fish (*Pantodon buchholzi*) both have deep bodies and powerful flapping pectoral fins that vibrate so fast in the air they create a buzzing sound. These "wings" are, however, relatively small and the flight is short, requiring a takeoff run of up to 40 feet, during which the fish is in contact with the water. When kept in an aquarium they will leap out if not kept covered.

There are many other species of fish that leave the water on short flightlike leaps to escape enemies or even to take insects, but seldom do such leaps exceed ten times the fish's body length, and they can never be considered either flight or gliding in the true sense.

Chapter 14
AMPHIBIANS AND REPTILES TAKE UP GLIDING

Parachuting Frogs

That a few amphibians should have developed into gliders seems natural when we realize how many frogs live in and leap about in trees. However, it is hardly to be expected that these could have evolved wings of a flapping nature. Nevertheless, some have developed parachutelike webs between their lengthened toes on all four feet. When they leap, these webs are expanded and brake the animal's descent into a glide.

Such gliding frogs are confined to Africa and Southeast Asia. The best known of them is rhacophorus, or *Polypedates spp.*, which can glide 30 to 40 feet from a height of 40 feet. The area of this frog's foot webs exceeds that of its body, and with its body flattened and the extended webs held closely against it, the area of what we might call its parachute is very considerable.

Hyla venulosa of Brazil is another frog which, although not a true glider, will launch itself from a height of 40 feet without coming to harm. Reptiles have necessarily developed different methods of gliding, and apart from the fact that birds have descended from ancient flying reptiles (see Chapter 11), no modern species of reptiles are able to fly. But several species glide.

41. *The gliding lizard* Draco volans *spreads its ribs and body membrane to create a parachutelike condition that enables it to glide up to 50 feet.*

Parachuting Lizards

A lizard, *Draco volans,* is typical of these. Found in the East Indies and Malaysia, it has no wings, but has evolved a unique parachute-like body structure that enables it to glide up to 50 feet. Its ribs can be extended outward for a greater distance than its limbs by the expansion of its body cavity, and by using this action to spread a body membrane, the animal can glide for considerable distances in the trees where it lives.

There is also a gliding gecko (*Ptychozoon homalocephalus*) that has a fringe membrane along the sides of its body and tail and between its digits, but this is not attached to movable ribs as in *Draco volans.*

Volplaners

Snakes would seem to be the least suitably constructed creatures for gliding, and yet there are some that can glide. These include *Ahaetula spp.*, *Chrysopelia ornata,* and *Dendrophis*. *Chrysopelia* is an Indo-Malayan golden tree snake that keeps its body rigid and makes the underside of its body concave by spreading its ribs like the lizard mentioned earlier so that it can volplane at an angle of about 45 degrees. It can travel for considerable distances, instantly contracting its body to a true cylindrical shape as it lands.

As specialized as these reptiles seem to be, they are not nearly so agile in the air as many of their ancestors were; nor are they so numerous.

Chapter 15

SOME MAMMALS
BECOME AIRBORNE

As we have seen with fish, amphibians, and reptiles, the term "flying" is not always appropriate when applied to those that can become airborne. This is so with many of the so-called flying mammals too. Some of them only glide; but bats do actually fly by flapping their wings like birds. They have been doing this for a long time, because fossils of bats that lived 60 to 65 million years ago have been found, and they were certainly well established 50 million years ago.

True Fliers

Bats' wings are hand membranes called *alar* membranes, which are webs of skin stretched between elongated fingers, and continuous with a side and tail membrane between the hind legs. The thumb is free and clawed, and it is used to grasp, but the other four fingers all support the wing membrane.

The bones of the arm are also elongated to play a part in this, and the rear part of the wing is supported by the short thigh and leg, but not the foot. In most, the tail is completely enclosed in the membrane; only in one or two species does it project slightly, and in one

42. *Bats' wings are* alar membranes, *skin webs stretched between elongated fingers, and continuous with hind legs and tail.*

or two others, like *Rhinopoma spp.* of Egypt, it extends to a considerable length. The foot has strong toes and claws with which the bat hangs when it is not flying.

The wing membranes are divided into three parts for descriptive purposes: a thin strip from the shoulder to the base of the thumb; the main part, the *patagium* (the wing), between the arm and the forefinger on the anterior side, and the arm and the hind limb on the posterior side; and between the spurs on each hind limb and including the tail, the *interfemoral* membrane.

Few bats can walk on the ground, and all are clumsy. But their flight is excellent, and very much like that of birds, the wingstrokes downward and forward and fully extended; then upward and backward with the wings partly folded and twisted. All these movements are aided by powerful chest muscles like those of birds.

Again as in birds, bats' wings vary in shape for different environments and speeds of flight. They vary in their frequency of beat, too, ranging up to 20 times a second according to species. Small bats with such fast wingbeats have extreme flight control and agility. Steering is accomplished in most by using a different strength of wingbeat on one side or the other.

A few bats can hover like hummingbirds, and they do this merely by changing their body angle upward so that they are virtually flying upward with just enough power to overcome gravity and so remain stationary. Some bats have such enduring powers of flight that they can make long migrations of up to 500 miles. Bats can therefore be said to be the only true fliers apart from birds.

Furry Gliders

Mammals that we must call gliders instead of fliers are of only two kinds, but these include quite a number of species, and they are widespread across the world. Flying phalangers are gliding marsupials confined to Australia, and these comprise a single group of three species. The other group includes two kinds of placental mammals: flying lemurs in the Philippines and Southeast Asia, mistakenly given this name because they have lemuroid faces; and flying squirrels, which are found in all parts of Southeast Asia, the Philippines, Taiwan, North and South America, and Europe. None of these have developed wings, and most are found in Asia.

The phalangers, two species of *Acrobates,* three of *Petaurus,* and one of *Schoinobates,* hardly ever descend to the ground. They glide for great distances between trees with the aid of a large membrane stretching from the neck to the hands, feet, and tail. They spread this membrane like a parachute as they launch themselves from a branch at a downward angle. When they land, they quickly climb again to gain the height necessary for the next glide.

The flying lemur, *Cynocephalus spp.,* acts exactly like the phalangers, has a similar parachute membrane, and can glide up to 70 yards. This animal also avoids the ground as much as possible; it cannot even stand up on the ground, but it can crawl fairly rapidly and makes for the nearest tree as fast as possible. Its fingers are not elongated like those of bats.

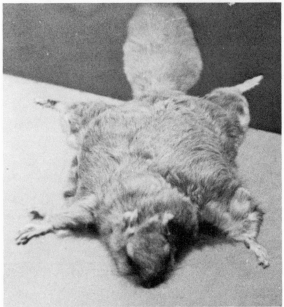

43. Top, *a marsupial phalanger from Australia spreading its skin membrane in a glide;* bottom, *a flying squirrel from North America doing the same thing.*

The flying squirrels, of which there are thirty-three species in twelve genera in Southeast Asia, one species in Europe, and three in America, all have similar gliding membranes to the phalangers and flying lemurs which carry them for considerable distances. These animals have relatively large hands, and their fingers are webbed, but not particularly elongated. They too climb very rapidly to regain launching height.

All of the gliding mammals—phalangers, lemurs, and squirrels—use their tails to some extent for steering, and in fact they exhibit an example of parallel evolution by which different animals in different parts of the world adopt similar structures and habits without necessarily being related, having common ancestors, or ever having any contact.

Chapter 16
INSECTS

The long history of the group of insectivorous vertebrates tells us that insects must have a longer history still, and the fact that there are almost a million species of insects in every kind of environment means they have been exceedingly successful. It is difficult to know just when insects first appeared on dry land; it may have coincided with the time when amphibians were the dominant inhabitants.

Winged insects, the only ones with which we are concerned here, are about 240 million years old, and they have been increasing in numbers ever since. Some scientists believe that the earliest insects were already winged, but this hardly fits evolutionary reasoning. One would expect at least gliding to precede flying, and some fossils discovered support this idea.

The Wings

Insect wings have evolved from outgrowths of the outer body skeleton or *integument,* and they are quite separate from the true limbs. Generally, insects have two pairs of wings, stiff lightweight membranes strengthened by a network of ribs or veins that are basically similar in all of them as far as the primary veins are concerned, but with other patterns of secondary veins that identify a species like fingerprints.

In some insects the forewings are harder and used as protective coverings for the others; and this is found in bugs, beetles, and grasshoppers. But most insects use both pairs of wings for flight. In many, the fore and hind wings are coupled together. This is clearly seen in cicadas, bees, and wasps. Bees even have small hooks on their hind wings that tie them to the forewings. In many flies and mosquitoes, however, the hind wings are so reduced as to leave virtually only one pair for flight, so these insects are called *diptera* (two-winged). However, a few of these have vestigial hind wings that have evolved into balancing stalks.

Most insects fold their wings over their backs when at rest, but dragonflies and mayflies keep them extended fully when at rest.

In nearly all insects the wings are operated mainly by vertical and horizontal muscles attached, not to the wings, but to the walls of the thorax. When the vertical muscles contract, the roof of the thorax is pulled down, and the wings flip up. When the horizontal muscles contract, the roof of the thorax is arched and the wings flip down. So the wings move up and down because alternate contractions of the flight muscles deform the thorax.

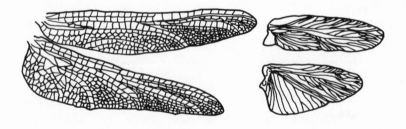

44. Left, *a drawing of the right pair of wings of a dragonfly, and* right, *the same of a cockroach. All are shown transparent, revealing the species-characteristic basic vein patterns.*

Flying Speeds

In many insects the flight muscles work at very high speeds. Here is a chart showing the rate of wingbeats per second and the wind speeds in miles per hour of some common insects:

mosquito	300 per second	2 miles per hour
housefly	200	5
white butterfly	12	6
honey bee	190	7
locust	20	10
dragonfly	25	18
horse fly	86	30
hawkmoth	70	35

There are other, smaller, muscles attached to the wing bases, which produce forward and backward movements and controlled inclination. The result is like a propeller. The insect is given both lift and forward movement.

The ability to fly at both low and high speeds seems to be difficult, if not impossible, for any particular insect. Each is restricted to one flying speed, even when hovering is possible. Because the principles of insect flight are similar to those of vertebrates, hovering like hummingbirds is quite possible to some of them; and those that do hover have similar diets to hummingbirds. They include nectar-drinking moths and syrphid flies, also known as hover flies.

Although it is considered that two-winged flies are the most efficient insect fliers, dragonflies can also be seen to have fast, skillful flight, with instantaneous change of direction and superb control. Unique sets of wing muscles make this possible, enabling them to fly as skillfully as any diptera. Their fore and hind wings are not coupled in any way, and they move alternately.

If one looks at a random selection of insects, the impression gained is that forewings are usually larger than hind wings, but in grasshoppers, cockroaches, katydids, crickets, and beetles, forewings are

45. Top, *a March fly (Tachinidae), in which the rear wings are quite vestigial;* bottom, *a chafer or scarab beetle (Scarabaeidae), in which the rear wings are the flight members.*

46. Top, *a dobsonfly* (Corydalus spp.), *which is essentially similar to a dragonfly in its wing form;* center, *a katydid* (Tettigoniidae), *in which the rear wings are predominant; and* bottom, *a luna moth* (Saturnidae).

47. Stick insects (Phasmidae), in which the forewings are almost vestigial.

more slender than hind wings, which are expanded, broad, and fan-like. Thus the hind wings are the principal flight wings. When not in use, they fold beneath the forewings, using these as covers.

Butterflies and moths use both pairs of wings, but their forewings are always the larger. Butterflies are slow fliers, but they can fly for a long time without fatigue. Moths are faster fliers, and this may be because their forewings and hind wings are yoked together to act as a single wing.

Legs

In nearly a million species of insects one would expect a great variation in all the organs of locomotion, but the principles of insect ground locomotion are much the same as in vertebrates. Insect legs, all of which are attached to the thorax, are adapted for walking, running, swimming, hopping, digging, climbing, grasping, and hanging upside down in various species. They all have three pairs of legs, hence are called *hexapods* (six-footed), and all of these legs move in direct sequence when used. Special adhesive claws and pads on many of them make it possible to walk in any position.

Each insect leg consists of five segments, some of which have been given names similar to vertebrate limbs. The short segment closest to the body and articulating with it is called a *coxa;* the next, the *trochanter,* is small and fused to a stout *femur.* Attached to this is a slender spiny *tibia,* and then the *tarsus,* which with three parts bears the claws and adhesive pads. It is the greatly developed tibia that is used for leaping.

The number and size of an insect's limbs govern the power and speed of its movement, the more robust of them performing more slowly, just as among vertebrates the movements of an elephant are slower than those of a gazelle.

We see another parallel with vertebrates in the similarities of grasshoppers, fleas, and so forth to kangaroos and hopping mice. All of these have greatly developed hind legs with unusually powerful muscles that enable them to leap many times their own length. There are a number of spiders that leap also, but these must walk like flies when going up and down a wall or across a ceiling.

Index

117